Library Searching:
Resources and Strategies

with examples from the environmental sciences

Library Searching: Resources and Strategies

with examples from the environmental sciences

Jacquelyn M. Morris and Elizabeth A. Elkins

State University of New York
College of Environmental Science and Forestry

Foreword by
Marta Dosa

Syracuse University School of Information Studies

ᏅᏢ

JEFFREY NORTON PUBLISHERS
145 EAST 49TH STREET, NEW YORK, N.Y. 10017

Library of Congress Cataloging in Publication Data

Morris, Jacquelyn M.
  Library Searching.

  Bibliography: p.
  Includes index.
  1. Libraries—Handbooks, manuals, etc.
  2. Searching, Bibliographical—Handbooks, manuals,
  etc. I. Elkins, Elizabeth A., joint author.
  II. Title.
  Z710.M67   029   77-9214
  ISBN 0-88432-004-9
  ISBN 0-88432-005-7 pbk.

Foreword

The book represents the insights, experiences and interdisciplinary literature search skills of the authors, reference librarians at the SUNY College of Environmental Science and Forestry (ESF) at Syracuse. The materials here included emerged from the curricular content of a library research course the authors have been giving to college juniors over the past several years. The working edition of the book, *Searching the Literature of the Environmental Sciences, a Strategy* was published by the ESF in 1976. It has become a popular aid to library research not only in the State University system, but also at other universities. It has been used by students in a variety of academic departments and professional schools, including schools of library and information science.

In both depth and scope, the present book goes beyond the parameters of a library instruction course, and may be greeted as a comprehensive approach to basic literature search strategy. The principles, definitions and information sources presented will be useful not only to students but also to educators and practitioners in a number of interdisciplinary fields.

Development of the Book

In 1973 the authors initiated the teaching of library research strategy to juniors at the SUNY College of Environmental Science and Forestry. The rationale for aiming the instruction at third-year students was to reach them at the point in their academic careers where they have a definite need for searching the literature. [1] The process of introducing such a course into the academic environment was a complex and challenging one. Many academic institutions look upon instruction in literature search methodology and resources as an informal corollary aspect of library service. However, more and more administrators and educators are becoming aware of the value of systematic information support throughout an individual's academic and professional life, and therefore promote formal credit courses in library research as an integral part of the curriculum.

The adoption of the formal program by the ESF faculty and administration represented the successful conclusion of an innovation process. It is briefly described here because it clearly reflects the transition from a fragmented, single-discipline-oriented approach to a comprehensive cross-disciplinary view of the information process.

First, the Public Services staff of the F. Franklin Moon Library at ESF conducted traditional course-related lectures and exercises for students of a few library-oriented faculty members. Next, the advantages of an interdisciplinary approach to the literature had to be proven. To this end the authors introduced a noncredit minicourse for third-year students. It was designed to help the student learn about the role of the library's organization and services, acquire literature search methods and become familiar with the typology and utilization of information sources. Data were collected on student progress by means of a pre-test and post-test. The data obtained in this pilot study supported the hypothesis that the approach and methodology of the course were effective. [2] In the following year, based on the experiment, ESF began to offer the innovative credit course on a regular basis, with expanded scope and objective. First, the course represents a change from a library-oriented view of the literature to a bolder concept which presents library research as part of the total information-gathering process. Second, from a focus on skills related to specific scientific fields the new program moves to encompass a cross-disciplinary approach to the environmental literature.

The program, as currently conceived, has a distinct behavioral orientation. It intends to sensitize students to the information process and to develop attitudes toward the utilization of sources. According to the authors' educational objectives, "The thrust of the program is to inculcate in the user skills, techniques, and attitudes which will facilitate user interaction with information systems." This understanding of the behavioral aspects of information gathering forms the foundation of the present book. It is significant because it raises the book above mere methodology and aligns it with the growing literature of interpersonal communication in respect to information utilization. Educators and environmental scientists are becoming increasingly aware of the role of communication strategies. A discussion and annotated bibliography on the topic in the *Journal of Environmental Education* may serve as examples.[3]

The authors' experience in designing the conceptual framework and collecting the information sources for the present book has been based on (1) a process to introduce an innovative educational program, (2) their familiarity with new developments in teaching search strategy, and (3) their grasp of the implications of interdisciplinary fields.

The Literature of the Environmental Sciences

The materials for this book have been developed at an academic institution which has undergone dramatic changes in recent years. The objectives, policies and curricula of the SUNY College of ESF were widened to include various aspects of environmental policy making, management, and research. This change process has been an integral part of national and global developments. For instance, a source at Yale reported in 1968: "By adopting an ecological approach, in conjunction with its traditional socio-economic orientation, the forestry school now stands at a frontier crossroad of the natural and social sciences, claiming a measure of authority in almost every area in which man interacts with the natural world." [4] Governments, especially in the industrialized parts of the world, recognized that "the environment could not be compartmentalized, for it is constituted by a network of interacting relationships extending through all sectors of human activity." [5]

In many countries, the mid-twentieth century saw a gradual change from public policy interests in conservation to growing concern with the whole spectrum of environmental problems. To be sure, the policy approach was still incremental and crisis-oriented. The enactment of the National Environmental Policy Act (NEPA) **of** 1969 was an indication, domestically, of a more comprehensive effort for policy formulation. In spite of the criticism this legislation has been drawing, it formed a much needed focus for academic, private sector, and citizen participatory movements. In 1972, the United Nations Conference on the Human Environment, in Stockholm, produced 26 principles and 109 recommendations in the "Declaration on the Human Environment." "Within the 109 recommendations for international action, 66 asked for exchange of information, 53 denoted areas of further research, and 30 indicated specific needs in training and education. All of these are dependent on libraries to fulfill their objectives. . . ." [6]

The great value of information as a resource for research, policy, and action has been recognized both at the national and international levels. At the First National Environmental Information Symposium in 1972, sponsored by the EPA, Congressional and regulatory information was repeatedly described as a social need shared by all sectors of the environmental field. Internationally, the United Nations Environment Programme was mandated to develop an International Referral System with focal points in all countries. The system is now developing directories of environmental information sources in order to refer inquiries to the national focal point or the source that is the most likely to have the needed information. These developments necessitate that librarians and other information practitioners place emphasis on environmental collections and search techniques.

Changes in the public sector have been paralleled by rapid developments at academic institutions. More and more colleges of forestry and agriculture have moved toward a broader interpretation of their field. Forest science, for instance, has been called upon to deal with resource allocation among competing land uses which affect the utilization of timber, mining practices, influence on industrial and residential development, or open-space recreation. The literature on the social responsibility of the planner, the landscape architect, and the architect is expanding. New interdepartmental courses and programs are emerging. They call for new cross-disciplinary information resources and skills.

Indeed, as a Task Force sponsored by the Rockefeller Brothers Fund reported, "the wave of environmental concern has been growing for decades, to the point where environmental awareness is now part of the conscious social concerns of virtually everyone." [7] The resulting proliferation of programs and information in research, the various areas of professional practice, and among public-interest-oriented groups inundate us by what one loosely terms environmental literature. The field includes knowledge generated by urban and regional planning, management, public administration, legal studies, the policy sciences, education, psychology, a wide spectrum of natural and life sciences, and numerous additional branches of the social and behavioral sciences.

How, then, may one define "environmental science"? Terms such as "ecology" and "the science of the quality of life" are not helpful enough in their current broad interpretation. One source defined "environmental science" as "basic and applied inquiry about changes in environmental quality resulting from the activities of man."[8] Many sources believe that a new ordered set of theories may emerge as the result of the current conceptual turmoil, but they vary in their opinion whether this crystallization process is a question of the near or far future. Almost all sources agree that environmental science attempts to inquire into human behavior as well as into physical environmental changes and their consequences. In view of this flux characterizing the field, the student needs clear and firm guidance to the literature. *This guidance is represented in the present book by an excellent set of strategies rather than by an exhaustive list of biblio-graphic titles. I believe that because of this approach, the book addresses itself to information seekers in any field, and it will not become rapidly outdated.*

Environmental Information

Environmental information is the process that transfers data and information from source to user in any field of knowledge or activity applicable to environmental problem-solving. Some of the characteristics of environmental information sources make especially crucial the teaching of literature search techniques and attitudes of communication. These characteristics include:

- The cross-disciplinary nature of research and professional work
- The differences in how people perceive problems and propose priorities and solutions
- Peaks and valleys in public-policy attention to these problems resulting in unevenness in the funding of research, information services, and collection development
- Scattering of the literature in almost all types of information resources, including indexing and abstracting services, directories, specialized biblio-graphies, government documents, statistical sources, etc.
- The need for the user to learn to interact with information sources and systems in order to determine the most useful search terms and definitions.
- The on-going proliferation of new information services and systems which mandate sound techniques of search and evaluation

These characteristics of the literature have lead the authors to certain assumptions which are responsible for what the present book offers:

1. It is important to shift the focus of library search methodologies from describing separate information sources in detail to an efficient understanding of how sources may be related to each other.
2. Information gathering principles and techniques will have an impact on the individual only if their roles in the educational and research process become clear to the information user.
3. The usefulness of both the information sources and the search strategies depend on how effectively the searcher is able to formulate an information problem and interact with services and systems.

Marta Dosa
Syracuse University
School of Information Studies

Notes to the Foreword

1. Morris, J.M., "Gaining faculty acceptance and support of library instruction: a case study." Paper presented at the 5th Annual Conference on library orientation and instruction, Eastern Michigan University, Ypsilanti, Michigan. Ann Arbor: Perian Press, 1975, p. 59.

2. Ibid, p. 64.

3. Dick, R.A., D.T. McKee, and J.A. Wager, "A summary and annotated bibliography of communication principles," *Journal of environmental education,* 5(Summer, 1974) 8-13.

4. "Finding the forest in the trees," *Yale Alumni Magazine,* 12:3 (Dec. 1968) 23.

5. United Nations Environment Programme, "Action Plan for the Human Environment: Programme development and priorities, report of the Executive Director," Geneva, April 2, 1973 (UNEP/GC/10).

6. Anglemyer, M., "Getting down to earth: the call of Stockholm upon the informational services," in Bonn, G.S., ed., *Information resources in the environmental services,* paper presented at the 18th Allerton Park Institute, November 12-15, 1972. Champaign-Urbana, University of Illinois Graduate School of Library Science, 1973, p. 116.

7. Barney, G.O., ed. *The Unfinished Agenda,* the citizen's policy guide to environmental issues. New York: Thomas Y. Crowell, 1977, p. 2.

8. Advances in Environmental Sciences and Technology, VI (1969), p. 1.

Dedication

To
Don and Jeanne
Nat and Clara

Acknowledgments

Permission to reproduce examples was granted as shown below:

The authors wish to thank the following people, without whose help the book would not have been written.

Donald F. Webster (Director of F. Franklin Moon Library at S.U.N.Y. College of Environmental Science and Forestry), who provided the guidance, encouragement, and administrative support that allowed us to write this book.

Dr. Robert Chambers, who gave us his consistent support.

All of our colleagues at Moon Library, who helped in many ways. We thank JoAnn Dionne for her comments and her contributions to the early developmental stages of this book. We thank Kay Rossi for her careful proofreading and Maria Pafundi for her editorial comments. We thank Dawn Bennett for typing the manuscript with patience and precision. We also thank Barbara Settel for compiling and verifying the list of references and helping with other revisions. And we give a very special thank you to Beth Ann Taylor for her proofreading, revising the "Selected List of Indexes and Abstracts," and compiling the index.

Finally, we wish to thank the students at E.S.F. who have helped throughout this project by offering their comments and criticisms, thus strengthening the book and enabling us to make it as thorough as it is today.

J. M. Morris
E. A. Elkins

Contents

Note to the Reader

Many kinds of information are found in academic libraries. Whether you are looking for specific data, locating a book, or reading reserve assignments, you will find that libraries play an important role in the educational process. In fact, using the library is usually essential when you are assigned a research or term paper. The process of locating and gathering information and published material on a topic is called a *literature search*. The primary goal of this book is to help you learn how to use the library effectively—by saving time and gaining proficiency in library skills—when doing a literature search.

If you have ever had any problems using a library or researching a topic, then this book should help you. *Library Searching: Resources and Strategies, with Examples from the Environmental Sciences* offers you strategies for systematically searching the literature and locating resources on a topic. You will learn to plan and implement an efficient search strategy using library, campus, and other information systems and to locate, evaluate, and select relevant materials.

Another objective of this book is to help you become independent in your search for information. It is hoped that by the time you finish the book you will feel that the mystique which has so long surrounded the library has been lifted. And hopefully the process will also reintroduce an important information source: the librarian.

The method of searching as outlined here is only one way to approach a literature search. In future searches you might rearrange this method, depending on how familiar you are with the topic and how exhaustive the search must be. In fact, you probably should modify this method to reflect your own style and work habits. *Library Searching: Resources and Strategies, with Examples from the Environmental Sciences* provides you with a systematic process that can be used to search most other types of literature. Once the strategy is learned, it can be applied to a search of the historical literature as well as the scientific literature. Although the examples are drawn from the environmental sciences, the authors recommend the strategy to any student interested in conducting a literature search in other areas, especially those which are interdisciplinary.

Some portions of this book may not be relevant to your immediate needs. However, study those parts of the process anyway, as one purpose of the book is to introduce you to as many parts of the information search process as possible. Even if a source does not seem relevant to your search, don't hesitate to give it a cursory look and make note of it for possible future use. The strategy presented here will not only help you to do research in college, but can also prove invaluable in later years. You may need to locate information at various times in your life. For example, you may use this strategy in professional research, avocations, community services, and public affairs work.

Each chapter begins with a set of key questions which serve as its objectives.

After completing the chapter, it would be wise to review these questions. Then, if some of the objectives are unclear, reread the appropriate sections. Some steps of the search strategy described in the book are flowcharted to clarify the process. Every attempt has been made to avoid the use of library jargon. However, if any of the terminology of the text is unfamiliar, turn to the glossary in the Appendix of the book.

The title of this book, *Library Searching: Resources and Strategies, with Examples from the Environmental Sciences,* deserves a brief explanation. Environmental science incorporates a number of disciplines. It is the study of all of life, and it also attempts to account for man's behavior in the world structure. An environmental scientist could be interested in chemistry, biology, ecology, forestry, urban planning, management, landscape design, conservation of natural resources, sociology, and all the areas within these general categories. The literature of environmental science spans the natural sciences as well as the social sciences and the humanities. Environmental science isn't one science but is a combination of many, and this book offers an interdisciplinary approach to the literature.

Chapter 1

Resource Literature and the Search Strategy

This chapter will answer these key questions:
1. What is the literature?
2. What is a literature search?
3. How is resource literature represented?
4. What are primary, secondary, tertiary, and nondocumentary sources?
5. Why is a strategy necessary for a literature search?
6. What is a research log and how is it helpful?

Libraries, as part of the information system, usually contain the written word in the form of books, periodicals, indexes, and other media. In recent years even the most traditional libraries have expanded their collections to include other forms of information—for example: microform, slides, tapes, records, and even computerized information-retrieval systems. In other words, libraries have grown to be much more than warehouses of books.

It has been said that knowledge is doubling every seven years. Even if we don't rely on these figures but think more conservatively, it is apparent that the increased amount of information makes retrieving a particular source both time-consuming and difficult. The fact that so much information is available and in so many forms makes using the library all the more complex.

It is vital for researchers to know what has already been done in their fields. They learn this by turning to records of observations and experiments of their predecessors. This record of earlier work on a subject is known as *its literature*. Locating this information is called *making a literature search*.

Literature can take a variety of forms. When initiating a search you should be aware of these forms so that you can fully understand what it is you are looking for and realize the many types of places you must search. This chapter will describe a number of forms that literature may take and will then further divide that literature into four types of sources.

Forms of Literature

Books

The most familiar form of literature is the book. Some kinds of single volumes or books are known as monographs. Some books are considered reference books because they are designed by their arrangement and treatment to be consulted for specific information rather than to be read consecutively.

3

Serials

A serial is a publication issued in successive parts at regular or irregular intervals and generally intended to be continued indefinitely. Serials may include the following:

1. *Periodicals.* A serial issued at regular intervals. Individual libraries generally have their own definition of a periodical, such as "a serial issued at least two times a year." Periodicals include magazines and journals such as *Newsweek, Architectural Record,* and *Journal of Forestry.*
2. *Annuals.* A serial which appears once a year (e.g., *Annual Review of Microbiology*).
3. *Annals.* A serial which records events of a year, transactions of an organization, or progress (e.g., *Annals of Botany*).
4. *Proceedings.* A published record of a meeting of a society or other organization.
5. *Transactions.* Published papers and abstracts of papers presented at a meeting of a learned society.
6. *Monographic series.* A series of individual books which also has a collective title, such as *Great Books on Administration.* These are often published by a university or society, although in addition they are frequently just a publisher's designation of a group of books.
7. *Review jornals.* Journals that contain review articles which synthesize and critically evaluate the significant research of a particular subject area. They usually contain extensive bibliographies.

   Directories, almanacs, and yearbooks may also come under the heading of serials.

Government Documents

Any publication originating in or printed with the authority—and at the expense—of any office of a legally organized government is a government document. State, federal, and foreign governments as well as the United Nations publish vast quantities of material on countless subjects. Government publications cover such diverse topics as law, how to make jelly, stream flow data, occupational information, and all subjects in between. Some government documents are serials, others are monographs or small pamphlets.

Pamphlets

A pamphlet is simply an independent publication (often a very small monograph or book) consisting of only a few pages, generally fewer than 50. Government publications are frequently pamphlets. Associations, organizations, companies, and other organized groups frequently publish pamphlets of significance to a researcher.

Theses and Dissertations

A research paper written in partial fulfillment of an advanced academic degree is a thesis or dissertation. These papers, compiled by one researcher, are often valuable to subsequent research in the same field or subject area.

Symposia

A symposium is a published collection of opinions on a subject. Usually it is the collection of papers of short addresses presented at a particular meeting on a specific subject. Symposia make the material presented at meetings and conferences available to those who were not there, and also provide the participants with a written record of the ideas and subjects presented.

Patents

A patent is a specification issued by a government to an inventor. It protects his or her exclusive rights to a design or process for a limited number of years. The length of time for the guarantee varies with individual countries. A patent is also the publication which contains the details of the design or process developed by the inventor.

Translations

Translations are renderings of publications from one language into another. Much of the important scientific literature is published in languages other than English—principally Russian, German, French, and Japanese. Translations of this literature are available in many forms, including complete versions of entire journals or articles, and simple summaries. These are several indexes to translations.

Annual Reports

An annual report is a document issued yearly by societies, institutions, agencies, or other organizations. Annual reports contain summaries of the official activities of the issuing agency for the year. They often include detailed budgets and other pertinent information.

Bibliographies

Bibliographies in general are lists of publications—books, articles, reports, documents, etc.—that are selected and organized around a particular theme. These lists may be limited by type of literature, author, place or date of publication, subject, or other categories. They may be comprehensive, or selective of only the best and most relevant literature.

Environmental Impact Statements

Environmental impact statements are documents prepared by a government agency to investigate the potential ecological and physical effects of its proposed legislation or activity. The conditions required for the undertaking of these statements are contained in the National Environmental Policy Act, 1970. The complete texts of impact statements are published and abstracts of statements are indexed in the *EIS: Key to Environmental Impact Statements.*

Guide to the Literature

A guide to the literature is a book giving the major sources of information for a particular subject area. It is usually arranged by types of sources (periodicals, abstracts and indexes, bibliographies). It also explains how to find and use the information contained in these sources.

Microforms

Microform is a general term for material which has been photographically reduced on film, paper, and other materials for machine reading. Microforms are available in the following types.
1. *Microfiche.* Photographic reductions of printed materials on flat sheets of film. Each sheet of film contains many frames which can, together, reproduce an entire article. Frames are read individually in reading machines.
2. *Microfilm.* Photographic reductions on cellulose film which can be of various widths and lengths. The film is wound around a reel and can be read with the aid of manually or electrically operated reading machines.
3. *Microcards.* Opaque cards of various sizes containing photographic reductions of printed materials. Material is arranged by frames, in rows, as on microfiche. It also must be read with the aid of a reading machine.

The Resource Literature*

Resource literature is generally divided into four types of sources: (1) primary sources, (2) secondary sources, (3) tertiary sources, and (4) nondocumentary sources. Each of these types is discussed in detail below.

The Primary Sources

Primary sources include the published original reports of research and scientific investigations. These sources represent new knowledge (or new interpretations of old knowledge) and constitute the latest available information. A piece of research is not considered complete until the results are made available to the scientific community. All details of the research should be described thoroughly so that the scientific investigation can be repeated (and therefore double-checked). Primary sources are found in many forms and include:
1. Monographs
2. Periodicals (many of which are devoted solely to reporting original work)
3. Conference proceedings
4. Patents
5. Theses and dissertations

---

*Adapted from: Grogan, Denis, 1973. **Science and Techonology: An Introduction to the Literature.**

While unpublished materials such as correspondence and laboratory note-books are considered primary sources, they are frequently inaccessible and therefore outside the mainstream of scientific literature.

Throughout your search you will be using a variety of sources. However, it is usually the primary source you want to consult for your research. All other sources serve as directors to or locators of primary source material.

Secondary Sources

Primary literature is widely scattered, disconnected, and unorganized. To overcome the difficult task of locating such sources, a second tier of information has developed, called *secondary sources.* These sources are compiled from primary sources and are arranged according to some definite plan. They represent "worked-over" knowledge, and they organize the primary literature in a convenient, accessible form. Secondary sources not only *repackage* the primary sources, but many of them have the further useful function of guiding the researcher to the original documents. Secondary sources which serve as locators for primary sources include:

1. Periodicals, a number of which specialize in interpreting and commenting on developments reported in the primary literature. Frequently these are termed *review journals,* and include such titles as *Annual Review of... Advances in...*
2. Indexing and abstracting services, which direct the researcher to specific periodicals or monographs.
3. Reference books, such as encyclopedias, dictionaries, handbooks, tables.

The literature search attempts to locate primary sources; the secondary sources are the tools of this search.

Tertiary Sources

The main function of this less well-defined group of sources is to aid the researcher in using both the primary and secondary sources. Tertiary sources include:

1. Directories
2. Certain types of bibliographies, such as:
   a. Lists of books (*National Union Catalog*)
   b. Location lists of periodicals (*New Serial Titles*)
3. Guides to the literature
4. Lists of research in progress
5. Guides to libraries and sources of information
6. Guides to organizations

Tertiary sources fit into your search strategy when you are attempting to locate many types of information. For example: use directories to locate an expert in your field; use a union list of serials to locate and retrieve a certain periodical; use a guide to organizations to locate an organization doing research in your field.

Nondocumentary Sources

Nondocumentary sources, often referred to as "the invisible college," form a substantial part of the communication system in the sciences. Although they are convenient, these services frequently vary in reliability. In many cases they serve merely as pointers to primary sources, or they may provide a chance to share ideas. These sources will become more and more a part of your private information-gathering process as you enter graduate school and/or your profession. They include:

1. Formal sources, such as:
   a. Research organizations
   b. Learned and professional organizations
   c. Industry, private and public
   d. Universities and colleges
   e. Consultants
2. Informal sources, such as:
   a. Conversations with colleagues, visitors, etc.
   b. "Corridor meetings" at conferences, etc.

It should be noted that some of the examples in these four lists overlap. For example, periodicals can be both primary and secondary sources. Other discussions of "literature" may list examples in another order or have a slightly different emphasis.

Search Strategy

For any research you attempt, whether in the chemistry laboratory or in the library, you should follow a *strategy*. That is, your research should be planned to eliminate the possibility of overlooking an important step. For example, failure to use the proper chemicals in the correct sequence will not bring about the desired reaction. A literature search is not unlike working in the chemistry lab. You need to consult the proper sources, and to gain the best results this should be done in a certain sequence.

The following section outlines a prototype for a strategy of an exhaustive literature search. The remaining chapters of this book amplify the outline. Many variations of this strategy are possible; many searchers, after gaining experience, alter it to better suit their work style. Depending on your familiarity with a topic, or on just how exhaustive you wish to make your search, the steps that follow may be rearranged or even eliminated.

A Search Strategy, Step by Step

1. *Learn about the library you are using.* Learn about the library at the beginning of your search. It can save you time! Ask a reference librarian to explain to you how the library is arranged. Often libraries have handouts, maps, etc., to help users orient themselves. (See "Library Basics," Chapter 2.)
2. *Select a general topic area.* Start by examining reference works. Dictionaries, encyclopedias, handbooks, will not only give you a synopsis or overview of

your general subject but may also suggest additional sources to consult later.

3. *Narrow your topic.* Now use all sources gathered thus far to clarify your topic in terms of scope, purpose, depth. (See "Topic Selection," Chapter 3.)

4. *Use the subject card catalog.* Use the library's list of subject headings to help you determine how to locate books on your topic. Make a list of key words or subject headings and then look for each one in the subject catalog. Read catalog cards very carefully. (See "The Subject Catalog," Chapter 4.)

5. *Retrieve monographic works.* When you have looked through the card catalog and identified all relevant books, retrieve them from the library collection. Examine all that are appropriate to your topic. Conduct a shelf search for additional material. (See "Retrieving Books," Chapter 5.)

6. *Review.* By now you have a general overview of your topic. Be critical and analyze your progress. Have you found more keys words or subject headings? Can you narrow or expand your topic? If you have found a wealth of information, should you consider narrowing your topic again? If you have found little material, remember you still have many other sources to consult.

7. *Refer to indexes and abstracts.* Use these sources to help identify serial literature. (See "Indexes and Abstracts," Chapter 6.)

8. *Retrieve serials.* Next, check the library catalogs to locate the materials you have just identified as being relevant. If your library doesn't have a particular article you need, you may want to submit an interlibrary loan request. (See "Locating Serials," Chapter 7.)

9. *Locate additional sources.* Government documents, pamphlets, newspapers, and the like, are frequently important to a literature search. Consult reference books if they are important to your search at this point. (See "Reference Books," Chapter 8.)

10. *Compile the bibliography.* Evaluate the material you have found in your literature search and include in your bibliography only that material which is relevant to your specific needs. Select and follow a style manual. (See "Compiling the Bibliography," Chapter 9.)

A Research Log

It is helpful to review and analyze your progress at every step throughout your search. Taking careful and complete notes will help in this evaluation. Your should keep a diary, or log of some sort in which you record your searching progress. These notes can play a vital role in your search strategy.

A research log gives you the opportunity to keep track of the specific steps taken in your search, as well as a place to record ideas and additional steps you plan to take. It is especially helpful if you are doing an exhaustive search, since over an extended period your sources, strategy, and ideas may become confused. Recording your thoughts and observations can also be helpful in subsequent literature searches. Keeping a log will help you monitor your progress; you can review what you have accomplished. It helps, too, to assure an orderly search because you can record exactly which sources have been searched, what information was found, and where.

A research log could be compared to a shopping list, or a list reminding you of errands to do. It also serves as a review of what has been done. A research log might include the following:

- Notes about your topic, and definitions of terms
- A clarifying paragraph about your topic
- A list of search terms
- Subject headings used in subject catalogs
- List of indexes and abstracts consulted, and a record of volumes and pages checked in each
- List of other sources or reference books checked
- Names of people contacted regarding your topic, and their responses
- Notes from any interviews with subject experts

Throughout this book suggestions will be made for specific items to include in your log.

Chapter 2

Library Basics

This chapter will answer this key question:

What are some questions to ask about a library before beginning a literature search?

The first step in the search strategy is to learn about the library you are using. Discovering what is available, in both services and materials, can help you throughout your search. Knowing where things are can save you time and possibly frustration.

Exploring the Library Step by Step

1. *Take a tour of the library.* Becoming familiar with the physical layout of the library is worth the effort. When working in the lab it pays to know what equipment is available and where it is stored. When searching the literature the library is your lab. Many libraries have self-guided tours. Taking one of these tours can be time well spent.

   Some of the areas to look for are a rare book room, archives, film library, microform readers, government document section, record collection, browsing collection, typing rooms, reserve area, reference and/or information desk, pamphlet file, display area, photocopiers, reading rooms (including any special reading areas, such as group or quiet study areas), current periodicals area, bound periodicals area, the stacks where books are kept.

   Discover whether the stack area is open to the public or closed to all but the library staff. How is the material arranged on the shelves? Are there other (branch) libraries with special collections on campus?

2. *Get acquainted with the librarians.* Even when you are familiar with the physical arrangement of a library and have a good search strategy to follow, there will be times when you need help. You many need to find a particular piece of information, or want advice on the best sources to consult, or instruction in the use of a special tool. The reference librarian is there to help you. Find out where the reference desk is and get to know the reference librarians. They can describe for you any special library services.

   Ask if there are subject bibliographers (librarians with expertise in a special subject) on the library staff. These librarians are also available to help researchers with their literature searches.

3. *Inquire about interlibrary loan.* Interlibrary loan is a cooperative agreement among libraries to loan materials to one another. If your library does not own the material you need for your research, it may be possible to borrow it from another library. A more detailed discussion of interlibrary loan appears in Chapter 8.

4. *Look for printed guides and/or information sheets about the library and its services.* Libraries frequently have printed material which describes the library, its sources, and its services. These guides may range from a simple bookmark to an elaborate handbook. A display area may be set aside for this information.

5. *Find the circulation area.* Most libraries have a circulation area. This is where you check out the books you borrow. Inquire about how this is done in your library. Do you need a library card? What are the loan periods and other regulations? Are there fines for overdue material?

6. *Inquire about the reserve reading area.* Academic libraries usually maintain an area where the faculty can set aside certain material to be read for class assignments. This area is usually separate from the main stacks and the loan period on this material is limited.

Chapter 3

Topic Selection

This chapter will answer these key questions:

1. How is a topic selected for a research or term paper?
2. How are potential topics evaluated and analyzed?
3. What is a literature summary and how can it help with topic selection?
4. What are search terms?

An effective researcher must be able to clearly delineate and isolate a problem for investigation. Choosing a topic is critical. The topic serves as a guide for determining what materials to include or exclude throughout the search. Selecting a topic for investigation is frequently the most crucial and difficult part of an assignment. Poorly chosen topics can result in wasted time and effort, unmanageable research, poorly organized papers, and, consequently, poor grades. Well-selected topics can help avoid these problems.

Topic selection is difficult unless you have some idea or starting place. A number of sources, however, can spark an interest in a topic. Class discussions, assignments, meetings, or anything you read can lead you to a subject to pursue. Begin with exploratory reading about a general or even vague idea; as you read, a more specific topic should develop.

When your paper or research is concluded it should be clear, orderly, and easy for readers to grasp and remember. It should also be accurate and complete. If the topic is not clearly defined in your mind, you will not be able to tell whether your paper is accurate and complete. How will you know what information to include or exclude? A well-chosen topic is like a yardstick. Use it to measure what to include and what to omit as you proceed through your search.

Selecting and Evaluating a Topic

In order to select a topic, it is helpful to develop criteria for analyzing and evaluating it. The following are criteria you could consider for measuring your potential topics.

1. *The topic should interest you.* The first consideration to give any possible topic is how interesting it is to you. You will be spending considerable time with it, and it is unwise to pick a topic in which you have little initial interest. Be sure you aren't merely settling on a convenient topic. If the subject is something about which you are biased, this is usually an indication of high interest. However, if you are prejudiced about the topic, approach it objectively.

2. *It should be manageable.* Be sure the topic is one you can handle. It shouldn't be too narrow or too broad. (The topic "mammals" would be too broad whereas "beavers in Onondaga County" might be too narrow.) Dealing with a topic requires flexibility. Keep in mind that as your research develops, changes will occur in the scope of your topic.
3. *It should be relevant.* A good topic, whether assigned, suggested, or chosen, should have significance for you and should, if possible, correlate with other courses and assignments. Don't pick a topic which is trivial or simply doesn't warrant your time. Keep the audience of your search in mind. Will the results be significant? Is your topic original and innovative? If an assigned topic is not particularly appealing to you, alter it to reflect your interests. Be sure to confer with your professor(s) concerning such a change.
4. *There should be sufficient information about it to suit the time available.* Consider whether or not you will be able to find sufficient information within the given length of time. After a preliminary search you may discover there is not enough material readily available, or not enough time within which to pursue it. Do you have a specific deadline or due date for your research? For example, do you really have the time to monitor the mating habits of beavers in Onondaga County? Similarly, if 200 citations are available with information on beavers, do any concern the beavers that inhabit Onondaga County?

   As you become more familiar with the search process and your searching skills develop, you will be able to do a quick preliminary search as you start any project. This will help you determine whether or not you will find enough information on the topic within the time allowed.
5. *It should suit your skills.* Be sure you have the skills necessary to complete the research on your topic. If your topic requires taking a survey, can you really do that effectively? Do you have a thorough knowledge of statistics, for example? If not, could your acquire it? Do you have the expertise to monitor the mating habits of beavers? Don't pick a topic which would be too technical for you. Is most of the literature published in a foreign language? Consider these potential problems objectively before making the final choice.
6. *It must be clear.* Whatever topic you choose, be sure it is clearly defined. Don't proceed with one that is vague or unclear. Your preliminary reading should help you define and gain an understanding of your topic's possibilities. However, you may begin your search for a general topic but then narrow it down as your research proceeds. If a subject is assigned to you, be sure you understand the assignment, especially any specific requirements or limitations.

Background Reading

Once you have selected a general topic, you may want to locate a *literature summary.* This is a general introduction, overview, or summary of a subject. These summaries review the information on a topic and usually point out basic sources to consult for further information. Review literature can be found in a basic text, an encyclopedia, or in sources known as *review journals.*

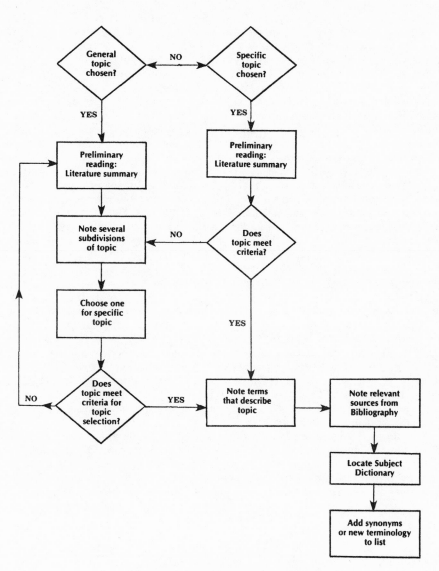

Figure 1. Topic selection flowchart

Review literature can help you define and delimit your topic by exposing you to the various aspects and dimensions of it.

There are several advantages to reading review literature. First, background material in a summary is usually general enough so that it is not easily outdated and can be used indefinitely. Even outdated material will provide historical information. In addition, a summary may include a bibliography for further reading. Special terminology, significant people in the field, as well as specific branches or subdivisions of general topic are often discussed.

A general book or text frequently offers a literature summary of a topic. To locate a text consult the subject card catalog under your general subject. Use a broader term if necessary (for example, look up "MAMMALS" if you can't find "BEAVERS"). Scan the cards under the general headings for your topic, looking for a basic book. Frequently a course textbook provides good background material for a literature search. Examine the table of contents for a chapter which deals with your general area of interest.

A general encyclopedia, such as the *Encyclopaedia Britannica,* or a subject encyclopedia, such as the *McGraw-Hill Encyclopedia of Science and Technology,* provides literature summaries. To find a general encyclopedia in the subject card catalog use the heading "ENCYCLOPEDIAS AND DICTIONARIES." Subject encyclopedias are listed under the subheading "DICTIONARIES," which accompanies a heading, like this: "SCIENCE—DICTIONARIES." When using an encyclopedia be sure to use the index volume to help locate your general topic. Ask a librarian to suggest a source if you are unable to locate one. (See Chapter 8, Reference Materials.)

You may also read a literature summary in a review journal. The articles in review journals comment and interpret information on a particular topic. Publications such as these include review articles: *Advances in Botanical Research, Progress in Bio-organic Chemistry, Current .Topics in Developmental Biology, International Review of Forestry Research.* A more complete list of review journals can be found at the end of this chapter. These sources are entered in the subject card catalog under the subheading "COLLECTED WORKS," like this: "BOTANY—COLLECTED WORKS." A valuable source which can lead you to review articles is *Index to Scientific Reviews.* A description of this index appears in the appendix.

A guide to the literature (which lists sources for the literature of a specific discipline, or subject area) may lead you to overviews, or summary sources. Try to locate a guide to your particular subject area, such as biology, chemistry, or geology, or refer to one of these two general guides: *Guide to Reference Books,* by Eugene P. Sheehy, and *Guide to Reference Material,* by Arthur J. Walford.

Search Terms

As you select your topic, begin a list of search terms. (Keep this list! You will use it again later.) A search term is the word or group of words under which material dealing with the same theme is entered in an index or catalog. Many times search terms are referred to as subject headings. Throughout your search the key to obtaining information will be these search terms. As you read a literature summary you will probably find some terminology that is unique or appropriate to your topic. Begin compiling your list as soon as you note terms significant to your topic; add to and modify the list as your search progresses.

Your ability to determine the best terms to search will become stronger as you proceed.

You may expand your list of search terms by using a subject dictionary if there is one appropriate to your topic. A subject dictionary defines terminology of a specific field. To locate these dictionaries, search under a broad term in the subject catalog, using the subheading "DICTIONARIES" (e.g., "ZOOLOGY—DICTIONARIES"). In this dictionary locate the words on your search term list, note the synonyms offered, and add them to your list. The dictionary can also—throughout your search—help to clarify any terminology which may be unfamiliar. (See Chapter 8, "Reference Materials.")

Since clarifying your topic is primarily a thought process, it might help to write a brief paragraph or extended title for it. This will enable you to clarify in your own mind what areas the topic does include as well as what it does not. It should clearly define your objectives and thus give you a better idea of what information you are looking for as you proceed through your search. Collecting all information that is remotely related to your topic doubles your task, as you will only have to sift through the collected material and then discard much of it.

Research Log

Begin to record your searching progress in your research log, as discssed in Chapter 1. At this stage your log might include a list of search terms, a clarifying paragraph or extended title for your topic, as well as other observations or notes you feel are important about selecting your topic. It could also include any sources you have consulted thus far—a review article, subject dictionary—as well as any sources listed in the bibliography of your literature summary.

Sources of Review Literature

Advances in Agronomy. 1949—Academic Press, N.Y.

Advances in Animal Physiology and Animal Nutrition (Fortschritte in der tierphysiologie und tierernaehrung). 1972—Verlag-Paul Parey, Hamburg, Germany.

Advances in Applied Microbiology. 1959—Academic Press, N.Y.

Advances in Biochemical Psychopharmacology. 1969—Raven Press, N.Y.

Advances in Biological and Medical Physics. 1948—Academic Press, N.Y.

Advances in Botanical Research. 1963—Academic Press, N.Y.

Advances in Chemistry Series. 1950—American Chemical Society, Washington, D.C.

Advances in Cell Biology. 1970—Appleton-Century-Crofts, N.Y.

Advances in Comparative Physiology and Biochemistry. 1962—Academic Press, N.Y.

Advances in Ecological Research. 1962—Academic Press, N.Y.

Advances in Environmental Science and Technology. 1969—Interscience Publishers, N.Y.

Advances in Enzyme Regulation. 1963—Pergamon Press, N.Y.

Advances in Food Research. 1948—Academic Press, N.Y.

Advances in Genetics. 1947—Academic Press, N.Y.

Advances in Geophysics. 1952—Academic Press, N.Y.
Advances in Insect Physiology. 1963—Academic Press, N.Y.
Advances in Marine Biology. 1963—Academic Press, N.Y.
Advances in Microbiology of the Sea. 1968—Academic Press, N.Y.
Advances in Parasitology. 1963—Academic Press, N.Y.
Advances in Psychobiology. 1972—Interscience Publishers, N.Y.
Advances in Pest Control Research. 1957—(1968)—Wiley, N.Y.
Advances in Study of Behavior. 1965—Academic Press, N.Y.
Advances in Water Pollution Research. 1962—Pergamon Press, N.Y.
Agricultural Science Review. 1963—Cooperate State Research Service, U.S.
    Department of Agriculture, Washington, D.C.
Annual Reports on Progress of Chemistry. 1904—Chemical Society, London.
Annual Review of Biochemistry. 1932—Stanford University Press, Stanford,
    Calif.
Annual Review of Earth and Planetary Sciences. 1973—Annual Review, Inc.,
    Palo Alto, Calif.
Annual Review of Ecology and Systematics. 1970—Annual Reviews, Inc.,
    Palo Alto, Calif.
Annual Review of Energy. 1976—Annual Reviews, Inc., Palo Alto, Calif.
Annual Review of Entomology. 1956—Annual Reviews, Inc., Palo Alto, Calif.
Annual Review of Genetics. 1967—Annual Reviews, Inc., Palo Alto, Calif.
Annual Review of Microbiology. 1947—Annual Reviews, Inc., Palo Alto, Calif.
Annual Review of Psychopathology. 1963—Annual Reviews, Inc., Palo Alto,
    Calif.
Annual Review of Plant Physiology. 1950—Annual Reviews, Inc., Palo Alto,
    Calif.
Annual Review of Psychology. 1950—Annual Reviews, Inc., Palo Alto, Calif.
Annual Review of Sociology. 1957—Annual Reviews, Inc., Palo Alto, Calif.
Bacteriological Reviews. 1937—Williams & Wilkins Co., Baltimore.
Biological Reviews. 1923—Cambridge University Press, London.
Biotechnology and Bioengineering. 1959—Interscience Publishers, N.Y.
The Botanical Review. 1935—New York Botanical Garden, Bronx, N.Y.
Chemical Reviews. 1924—American Chemical Society, Washington, D.C.
Chemical Society Reviews. 1972—Chemical Society, London.
Chemical Zoology. 1967—Academic Press, N.Y.
CRC Critical Reviews in Biochemistry. 1971—Chemical Rubber Co., Cleveland,
    Ohio.
Critical Reviews in Environmental Control. 1970—Chemical Rubber Co.,
    Cleveland, Ohio.
CRC Critical Reviews in Food Technology. 1970—Chemical Rubber Co.,
    Cleveland, Ohio.
CRC Critical Reviews in Microbiology. 1971—Chemical Rubber Co., Cleveland,
    Ohio.
Current Advances in Ecological Sciences. 1975—Pergamon Press, N.Y.
Current Topics in Bioenergetics. 1966—Academic Press, N.Y.
Current Topics in Developmental Biology. 1966—Academic Press, N.Y.
Interdisciplinary Science Reviews. 1976—Heyden & Sons Ltd., London.
International Review of Forestry Research. 1964—Academic Press, N.Y.
International Review of General and Experimental Zoology. 1964—Academic
    Press, N.Y.

Methods of Animal Experimentation. 1965—Academic Press, N.Y.
Oceanography and Marine Biology, An Annual Review. 1963—Hafner
    Publishing Co., N.Y.
Progress in Biophysics and Molecular Biology. 1950—Pergamon Press, N.Y.
Progress in Oceanography. 1963—Pergamon Press, N.Y.
Progress in Organic Chemistry. 1952—Butterworths Scientific Publishers,
    London.
Progress in Physical Organic Chemistry. 1963—Interscience Publishers, N.Y.
Progress in Planning. 1973—Pergamon, N.Y.
Progress in Theoretical Biology. 1967—Academic Press, N.Y.
Progress in Water Technology. 1972—Pergamon, N.Y.
The Quarterly Review of Biology. 1962—Stony Brook Foundation, State
    University of New York, Stony Brook.
Residue Reviews. 1962—Academic Press, N.Y.
Science Progress. 1906—J. Murray, London.
Survey of Biological Progress. 1949—Academic Press, N.Y.
Symposia of the International Society for Cell Biology. 1962—Academic Press,
    N.Y.
Symposia of the Society for Experimental Biology. 1951—Academic Press, N.Y.
Symposia of the Zoological Society of London. 1960—Academic Press, N.Y.
World Review of Animal Production. 1965—World of Animal Producers, Rome,
    Italy.
World Review of Pest Control. 1962—Fisons Pest Control Ltd., Cambridge,
    England.

Chapter 4
The Subject Catalog

This chapter will answer these key questions:

1. What is a card catalog and how is it used when researching a topic?
2. What are subject headings?
3. How is the *Library of Congress Subject Headings* used?
4. Why is it helpful to understand the various parts of a catalog card?
5. What are bibliographic cards and how are they useful in a literature search?

A library's catalog is the primary index to its collection and therefore it is basic to one's knowledge in libraries. The fundamental principles of the catalog can be applied to many of the sources to be used later in the search strategy. Consulting the catalog is a good place to begin a search because you can determine what books the library has on your topic. This chapter will describe library catalogs and explain how they should be used in your literature search.

Library Catalogs

There are several kinds of library catalogs but the kind most commonly found in college and university libraries is a *card catalog*. As the name implies, this catalog is a group of cards, filed in an alphabetical arrangement, and kept in drawers. Each card in the drawer represents a book or group of books in the library. Each 3-x-5 card tries to describe as completely as possible the book it represents.

Library catalogs may also be in book form. In that case, rather than searching through cards the user scans volumes of books which contain entries much the same as those on catalog cards. Some specific examples of book catalogs will be described in the next chapter.

In a card catalog, books are usually represented (i.e., given an entry) more than once. Most books are entered at least by author, by title, and by subject. There can be additional entries for joint authors, series, or for additional subjects which are thoroughly treated in a book. It is possible for one book to be represented five or six times. Card catalogs come in many styles, but the two most common are *the dictionary catalog* and *the divided catalog*.

A dictionary catalog has all types of entries (author, title, subject) filed together. For example, cards representing books *by* Darwin and books *about* Darwin would be found in the same catalog. You can usually differentiate *subject entries* because their *headings* are typed in capital letters or in red type.

A *divided catalog* separates the types of entries into different sections, essentially making two or more catalogs. Usually a divided catalog has two

21

parts—the author/title and the subject. Author entries and title entries are kept in the author/title catalog. Example: Books by, or pertaining to, Darwin, and books with "Darwin" in the title, would be filed here. Subject entries are filed in the subject catalog. Example: Books with Darwin as the subject would be represented here. Dividing the catalog usually makes searching easier. If you know the exact title or author's name, you can check the author/title part of the catalog. However, if you want to know what books the library has on your topic, you can check the subject part.

Libraries frequently have more than one catalog. They may maintain catalogs for separate collections within the library. For example: serials, government documents or films. These separate catalogs may be located with the collections they represent or with the main catalog. They may also be a duplication of cards in the main catalog that are merely reproduced in a separate catalog for the user's convenience.

Subject Headings

The subject catalog, which provides access to the library's collection by subject, uses standardized words or headings, and is arranged according to a uniform system. All libraries rely on some system of *subject headings* and use a prescribed format for arranging information on catalog cards. Most college and university libraries use a list of subject headings developed by the Library of Congress (LC) in Washington D.C. This system had been adopted for two reasons. First, it allows patrons to go from library to library without having to learn a new system each time, and second, it saves individual libraries from having to develop their own systems. There might be minor differences among libraries, but the fundamental system remains the same. By becoming familiar with the library's subject headings you will be able to make the best use of its collection and avoid several days of aimless browsing in the stacks.

The *Library of Congress Subject Headings* serves as an index to the subject headings which are used in the card catalog. This list of headings is important because it:

1. Tells the user under what headings a given subject may be found in the catalog.
2. Directs the user to other headings which may be relevant.
3. Breaks the subject into several parts, helping the user limit the subject.
4. Ensures consistency of subject headings. A heading used for one book on a particular subject will be used for all other books on that subject.

Subject headings may be one of many types, for example:

- A word: "HORTICULTURE"
- A phrase: "FORGIVENESS OF SIN"
- A compound heading which makes a concept more specific and expresses a relationship between two concepts: "EDUCATION, HIGHER"
- A person: "WRIGHT, FRANK LLOYD"

A subject heading may have a subdivision which amplifies the heading. A list

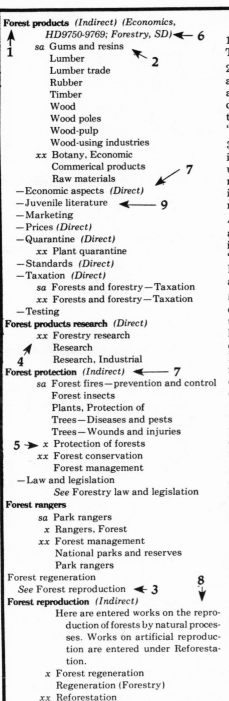

Forest products *(Indirect)* *(Economics,*
HD9750-9769; Forestry, SD) ◄— **6**
   sa Gums and resins
      Lumber ◄ **2**
      Lumber trade
      Rubber
      Timber
      Wood
      Wood poles
      Wood-pulp
      Wood-using industries
   xx Botany, Economic
      Commerical products
      Raw materials ◄— **7**
 —Economic aspects *(Direct)*
 —Juvenile literature ◄——— **9**
 —Marketing
 —Prices *(Direct)*
 —Quarantine *(Direct)*
   xx Plant quarantine
 —Standards *(Direct)*
 —Taxation *(Direct)*
   sa Forests and forestry—Taxation
   xx Forests and forestry—Taxation
 —Testing
Forest products research *(Direct)*
   xx Forestry research
      Research
4   Research, Industrial
Forest protection *(Indirect)* ◄——— **7**
   sa Forest fires—prevention and control
      Forest insects
      Plants, Protection of
      Trees—Diseases and pests
      Trees—Wounds and injuries
5 ► *x* Protection of forests
   xx Forest conservation
      Forest management
 —Law and legislation
     See Forestry law and legislation
Forest rangers
   sa Park rangers
   x Rangers, Forest
   xx Forest management
      National parks and reserves
      Park rangers
Forest regeneration
  See Forest reproduction ◄ **3**   **8** ↓
Forest reproduction *(Indirect)*
      Here are entered works on the repro-
        duction of forests by natural proces-
        ses. Works on artificial reproduc-
        tion are entered under Reforesta-
        tion.
   x Forest regeneration
      Regeneration (Forestry)
   xx Reforestation

Key

1. Boldface type indicates a heading. Therefore "Forest products" is a heading.

2. "sa" means "see also," which suggests another heading that is also used. In addition to the heading "Forest products," the user is advised to "see also" the headings: "Gums and resins," "Lumber," "Lumber trade," etc.

3. "See" is a direction to another heading, i.e., away from a heading which is *not* used to one which *is* used. "Forest regeneration" is *not* a heading. The user is being told to see the heading "Forest reproduction."

4. "xx" means "see also from," which is a direction from another heading which is used. Users seeking the heading "Forestry research," "Research," or Research, Industrial" are directed to see also "Forest products research."

5. "x" means "see from," which is a direction from a heading which is *not* used to a heading which *is* used. Users looking for "Protection of forests" are directed to see "Forest protection." Remember that "x" and "xx" are primarily designated for a library cataloger, one who assigns subject headings. They enable the cataloger to put "see" and "see also" notes in the card catalog. The user needs only to remember that words prefaced by "xx" are other headings to consult and those prefaced by "x" are not.

6. With many headings a general LC classification number is given which generally represents the most common aspect of a subject. This provides for browsing through a subject area.

7. "Direct" and "Indirect" are directions for the cataloger to follow when assigning subdivisions to a subject heading.

8. A scope note, such as the one listed under "Forest reproduction," specifies the range of subject matter to which the heading is applied by drawing necessary distinctions between related headings or by stating which of several meanings of a term is the one used in the list.

9. Subdivisions are indicated by a dash (e.g., "Forest products—Juvenile Literature").

Figure 2. Sample column, Library of Congress subject headings

of subdivisions which may be used with subject headings can be found in the introductory pages to the *Library of Congress Subject Headings*.

- Form: "LANDSCAPE ARCHITECTURE—PERIODICALS"
- Place: "FORESTS AND FORESTRY—CALIFORNIA"
- Time: "ARCHITECTURE, MODERN—20TH CENTURY"
- Topic: "ECOLOGY—STUDY AND TEACHING"

There are a few practical notes to remember about subject headings:

- Subject cards are filed alphabetically by the subject heading, which is typed in capital letters across the top of the card. All books with the same subject heading are then arranged alphabetically by author.
- There is a time lag before the terminology used in the latest books on a subject is added to the LC subject heading list and, consequently, the subject card catalog. This is due to the expense and confusion involved in changing subject headings in a large library, particularly when new phrases may drop out of use within one or two years. So if your topic is of current interest, or is undergoing a revival of interest, you may find materials listed under older, seemingly outdated terms.
- When using the *Library of Congress Subject Headings* and the subject card catalog itself, begin by looking for the most specific heading you can think of which covers your subject. If you do not find that heading, look under a more general one.
- Every catalog card has a list of all the subject headings under which this work can be found in the catalog. This list, called tracings, appears on the bottom of each card and is prefaced by arabic numbers. There are two ways to use the tracings in a subject search (see Figure 4).

1. Because every subject which is fully discussed in a book should have a subject entry, the tracing will give you a further indication of the book's content.
2. If the book seems appropriate to your needs, the other subject entries in the tracing might also be appropriate to your search. Add relevant headings to your search term list.

Figure 2 shows a sample column from the *Library of Congress Subject Headings* on the left, with explanation on the right. A detailed explanation of the Library of Congress list appears in its introductory pages.

Procedure for Using Library of Congress Subject Headings

1. List each term you have thought of or read that might be a descriptor of the topic.
2. Look up these terms in the *Library of Congress Subject Headings*.
3. If you find your search term in boldface type (number one in table) it is used by the Library of Congress ("accepted") and can be used to access the card catalog.
4. Check this "accepted" term for further leads by noting if it is followed by

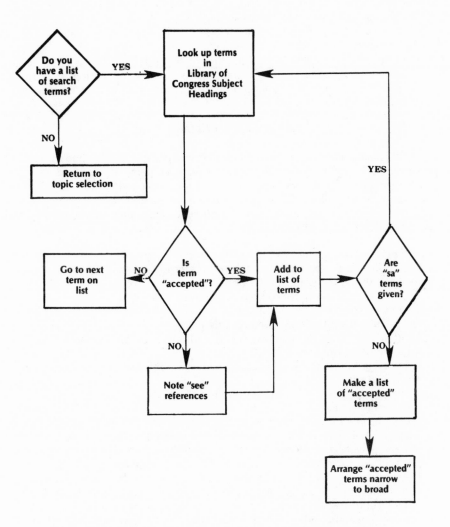

Figure 3. Library of Congress subject headings flowchart

an "sa" (Number two on the table).

5. If "sa" are listed, add those which seem relevant to your topic.
6. If the term you have looked up is not in boldface print, then it is not an "accepted" term. However, your term may be followed by a "see" reference (number three on the table).
7. If the term listed as a "see" reference seems relevant, follow up on this new term.
8. If the search term from your original list is not mentioned at all then proceed to the next term on your list.
9. Follow through with each term on your original list plus all new terms gained through the use of "see" and "sa."
10. Your final product should be a list of terms relevant to your topic and "accepted" by the Library of Congress for use in card catalogs that use the LC system. These terms should be listed from specific to general for your search of the card catalog.

Anatomy of a Catalog Card

Each catalog card is an abbreviated representation of the book's content. Learning to interpret the meaning of the various parts of the card can save time. Rejecting an irrelevant book at this point in the search can save a trip to the stacks, and in a large library that trip could take quite a bit of time.

Figure 4 shows a typical entry in the subject card catalog. The various parts of the card are as follows:

Call number—indicates book's location in the library
Subject heading—indicates the subject matter of this entry
Author—shows the writer of the book
Author's birthdate—is *not* to be misinterpreted
   to mean the date of publication
Title—includes subtitle as given on title page
Joint author—gives the name(s) of any additional person responsible for
   the writing of the book
Imprint—is the place of publication, name of publisher, and date of
   publication
Collation—gives a physical description of the book—number of pages,
   illustrations, and size
Series statement—gives the name of a series to which a book belongs;
   ordinarily it follows the collation and is enclosed in parentheses
Notes—gives added information that is often helpful to the researcher. In
   this case it points out that a bibliography is included
Tracings—lists all added entry headings under which the work may in theory
   be found in the catalog. An added entry is any entry other than the main
   one. There may be added entries for title, subjects, series, translator, etc.
   Subject headings are numbered with arabic numerals; entries which appear
   in the author/title catalog are numbered with roman numerals.

Bibliographic Notes

As you come across entries in the subject catalog for books that are relevant to your topic, you should take careful notes. A bibliographic note card which

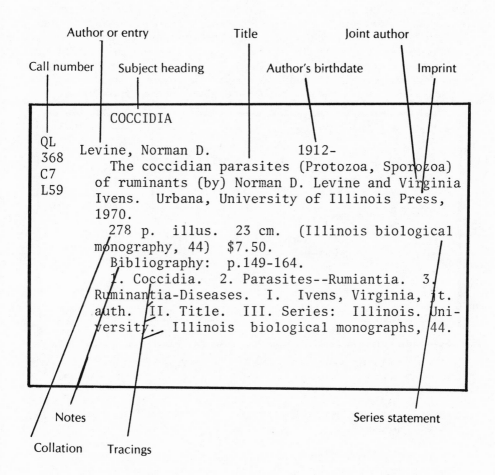

Figure 4. Subject catalog card

records the complete bibliographic citation from the catalog cards is important to the entire search. Backtracking later to relocate an incomplete citation is time-consuming and frustrating. A bibliographic card should be completed for every piece of material examined, even those eventually rejected.

These cards may be filed a number of ways, depending on where you are in your search. In the early stages you may keep them in alphabetical order. This will allow you to check through the quickly as you add each new citation just to be sure it is not an item you have already consulted. As you prepare to retrieve the books from the shelves, you may want to rearrange the cards into call number order. Later, when you have sorted out those books and articles you wish to include in your bibliography, you may rearrange them once more into alphabetical order and type a bibliography directly from the cards.

EMMEL, THOMAS C.	Call Number
Author	and Source
AN INTRODUCTION TO ECOLOGY &	QH
Title POPULATION BIOLOGY	541
	E45
	MAN - INFLUENCE ON NATURE
Serial or Periodical	
N.Y. W. W. NORTON & Co. INC.	
City Publisher	
1973 196	
Year Volume Pages	
OK FOR BASIC INTRODUCTION, GLOSSARY, SMALL	
Remarks BIBLIO. NOT VERY SPECIFIC.	

Bibliographic note card for monograph (book)

These cards should be consistent in their arrangement and should contain the following information:

1. Author's full name, last name first.
2. Full title of the book (don't abbreviate).
3. Series and volume number, if there is one.
4. Place of publication, name of publisher, and date of copyright
5. Number of pages in book
6. Call number. (Combination of letters and numbers in upper lefthand corner of catalog card).
7. Location symbol or library
8. How you found this reference. For example: Card catalog under "FOREST MANAGEMENT—N.Y. STATE"
9. One critical remark, such as:
   "very detailed analysis"; "statistics, graphs and charts"; "of immense value"

10. *Note:* Even books of no value should have a card—with the evaluation noted. Later in your search you may find a reference to the same work and you can check your bibliographic file to see if you have already looked at this source. This will save you another trip to the stacks.

Subject Search Process

Searching the subject catalog requires a systematic approach. Starting with the A's and going through the alphabet would be just as time-consuming as browsing aimlessly in the stacks. Therefore, a systematic but flexible approach—that allows for several ways of locating books on your topic—is best. Frequently, librarians are asked, "How can I tell if I have found everything the library has on my topic?" or "When is my search finished?" These aren't easy questions to answer. First it depends on what type of information you need. If you simply want the height of Mt. Everest, then your search will be completed when you locate the specific number of feet. However, if you want to do an exhaustive search on a specific topic, the answer is more complex. The process described here is one method of being fairly sure you have completed an exhaustive search of the monographic material available in your library.

If, after searching the subject catalog, you haven't found much information, don't be too concerned. This is not necessarily an indication that the library does not have the information you need. It might mean the information is not in book form. It could be in journals, especially if the topic you are searching is relatively new. Locating serial literature will be covered in later chapters. If you are overwhelmed with information, you should consider reevaluating your topic, perhaps considering a smaller aspect of the subject. There might be a problem also with your search technique—that is, you might be using search terms that are too broad.

Review of the Subject Catalog Search

1. Make a list of search terms. You started a list in Chapter 3. Now add any new terms you think of or that you found in your preliminary reading. Consult the *Library of Congress Subject Headings* and note which of these terms you can use to search your topic in the subject catalog. Make use of the "see" and "see also." List the narrow terms first, then the broader terms.
2. Begin your search with the narrow terms, then use the broader terms. This allows you to pick up what specific information the library has on your topic first.
3. Note all revelant books and call numbers.
4. Note the tracings on the cards that represent relevant books. If these search terms aren't on your list, add them now.
5. Using these additional search terms which were found as tracings, search again through the subject catalog. Add any relevant meterials to your bibliographic notes.
6. Record your steps and progress in a research log.

Chapter 5
Retrieving Books

This chapter will answer these key questions:

1. What are call numbers and how are they interpreted?
2. What is a shelf search?
3. What are some important filing rules to remember when you are using the card catalog?
4. What criteria can be used to evaluate a book?
5. What tools—in addition to card catalog—can be used for locating books on a topic?

After you have identified useful entries in the card catalog, your next step is to locate the material in the library's collection. The book's call number, a combination of letters and numbers in the upper lefthand corner of the card, indicates where the book can be found. This chapter will describe how to locate books by using their call numbers, how to systematically search the shelves for additional materials and how to evaluate books once they are located.

Classification

Materials in a library must be physically organized in some way so they may be found easily. Organizing materials, grouping them by subject, and assigning numbers to keep these subjects together, is known as classification. There are two commonly used classification systems in this country: the Dewey Decimal classification, perhaps the most familiar since it is used in many school and public libraries, and the Library of Congress classification system, which is used in most colleges, and university and research libraries.

The purpose of the LC classification system, which uses a combination of letters and numbers, is to group books by subject and to provide a location symbol (a call number) for each book in the collection. The LC call number consists, in general, of two principal elements: a class number and a book number. Other symbols may or may not be added to designate a particular title and a particular edition (see Figure 5).

Each of these letters or group of letters represents a subject area or a class. For example, Q represents science and S represents agriculture. By adding a second letter the class is further refined. Thus, QA is that field of science known as mathematics, and QH is natural history.

To place together all books on a specific subject the class letters are further divided by numbers. Thus, QH 540 is ecology and QH 573 is cytology.

31

When the books are shelved, the call numbers are arranged first by class number and then by book numbers. Class numbers are arranged alphabetically and numerically:

BF	HD	HD	Q	QK	S	SF	SH	SH
31	996	9868	150	85.5	120	199	377	377.5

Book numbers are arranged decimally:

QK	QK	QK	QK	QK	QK	QK	QK
85.5	85.5	85.5	85.5	85.5	85.5	85.5	85.5
A35	B55	B6	M46	M5	O3	O315	R55

QK	QK	QK
85.5	85.5	85.5
R8	S771	S78

A—General works
B—Philosophy
C,D—History
E—History
F—History
G—Geography
  GB—Physical geography
  GC 1080-1572—Marine pollution
  GV—Sports and amusements
    (outdoor recreation)
H—Social sciences
  HC 79—Environmental policy
  HM 206—Environment (Sociology)
  HV 6150-84—Environment and crime
J—Political Science
K—Law
  KF 3775—Public health (Law)
    Including environmental
    pollution
L—Education
M—Music
N—Fine arts
  NA—Architecture
  NG—Graphic arts
P-PZ—Language and literature
Q—Science
  QA—Mathematics
  QC—Physics
  QD—Chemistry
  QE—Geology
  QH—Natural History
    QH 301-705—Biology
    QH 540—Ecology

QH 543.5-6—Environmental radioactivity (Ecology)
QH 545—Environment effect on plants and animals
QK—Botany
  QK 746-759—Plants
QL—Zoology
QP—Physiology
  QP 82-82.2—Animals
QR 97—Environmental factors (Microbiology)
R—Medicine
  RA 565-602—Environmental health
S—Agriculture
  SD—Forestry
T—Technology
  TA—Envineering (general)
  TA 170-171—Environmental engineering
  TD—Environmental technology
  TD 172-TD 190.7—Environmental pollution
  TD 420-427—Water pollution
  TD 878-879—Soil pollution
  TD 881-890—Air pollution
  TD 891-893.5—Noise pollution
  TK—Electrical engineering
  TP—Chemical technology
  TR—Photography
  TS—Manufacture
U—Military Science
V—Naval Science
Z—Bibliography

Figure 5. Abridged outline of major classes of the Library of Congress classification system (emphasis on environmental areas)

Additional information is sometimes found in a call number. When it is, it is indicated as shown in the following examples:

1. When date of publication is part of the call number, books are shelved in chronological order.

Examples: S   S
             591   591
             A24   A24
             1964   1972

2. When the library owns more than one copy of the same book, this is noted as part of the call number:

Examples: S   S   S
             591   591   591
             A24   A24   A24
             1972   1972   1972
                        c.2   c.3

3. Frequently libraries add still another item to the call number—the *location symbol*. When this letter, symbol, word, or group of letters or words is used with the call number it further indicates where a book is shelved. If you are using the catalog of a large university library system these location symbols may sometimes indicate in which branch library the material can be found. Note this symbol carefully. It can save you many steps.

Shelf Search

Once you have indentified your call numbers, you locate the books by searching the shelves. As noted before, you can arrange your bibliographic note cards in call number order to ensure an orderly search.

The class number groups books on the shelf by subject, and as you use the LC classification system you will find call numbers falling into one or more groups of numbers. For example, books on wildlife ecology will be found in the QL 351's and SK 351's. Classification numbers will probably not be identical from library to library because the book number might differ. However, knowing the general class numbers allows you to go into any library that uses the same classification system and immediately locate the books on your subject.

Remembering that the LC classification system groups books by subject, it is possible to do a *shelf search* for additional material. "Doing a shelf search" simply means examining the books on either side of the book you have gone to look for. It is likely that these books will also be relevant to your topic. A shelf search can be helpful in finding books that were overlooked in the subject catalog. However, books may of course be off the shelf at a given time and thus certain materials may continue to elude you. A *shelf list* may be able to help you.

Shelf List

Libraries frequently have another card catalog, arranged in the order in which the materials are placed on the shelves—that is, arranged in call number order. This special catalog is called a *shelf list,* and if it is accessible to you it can expedite your search. Then, rather than doing a shelf search, and missing books that are off the shelf, you can search the shelf *list*. This list indicates all the books that are scheduled to be on any shelf, no matter where they may actually be at the time. Therefore, although you may not be able to find the actual material at that moment, at least you will know it exists.

If, through the shelf search—or by searching the adjacent cards in the shelf list—you locate additional materials, you should take another step. Look up each of these new sources in the author/title catalog and examine the tracings of entry (the tracings are the list of subject headings). If the tracings are new to your search term list, then add them. With these new terms repeat the search process.

Author/Title Catalog

Books can be entered in the author/title catalog in many ways. The following examples give you some indication of the range of possibilities.

Publications issued by government agencies are usually entered under the name of the government first, then the smallest distinctive unit. However, determining the correct way to look for a government agency can be difficult. If after checking the obvious ones you are unsuccessful, ask a reference librarian for help.

```
QL
971    Beatty, Richard Alan.
B36         Parthenogenesis and polyploidy in mammalian
       development. Cambridge [Eng.] University Press,
       1957.

            xi, 131 p. illus. 22 cm. (Cambridge monographs
       in experimental biology, no.7)

            Bibliography: p.114-127.


            1.Parthenogenesis (Animals) 2.Polyploidy.
       (Series)
                                               A 58-3482

       Arizona. Univ.     O
       Libr. for Library of Congress  [60u10]
```

Author card, entered by personal author

```
Ref.        Neebe, David J. 1929-              joint author
SD
393    Marty, Robert Jay, 1931-
M33       Compound interest tables for long-term plan-
       ning in forestry, by Robert Marty and David J.
       Neebe. Washington, U.S. Forest Service;[for sale
       by the Supt. of Docs., U.S. Govt. Print. Off.]
       1966.

          ii, 103 p. 29 cm. (Agriculture handbook no. 311)
          $0.70

          1.Interest and usury-Tables, etc. 2.Forests and
       forestry-Tables and ready-reckoners.  I. Neebe,
       David J., 1929- joint author, II. Title, (Series:
       U.S. Dept. of Agriculture handbook, no. 311)

          SD393.M33              511.8           Agr66-242
```

Joint author card, entered by joint author

```
Ref.        Compound interest tables for long-term plan-
SD                ning in forestry
393    Marty, Robert Jay, 1931-
M33       Compound interest tables for long-term plan-
       ning in forestry, by Robert Marty and David J.
       Neebe. Washington, U.S. Forest Service;[for sale
       by the Supt. of Docs., U.S. Govt. Print. Off.]
       1966.

          ii, 103 p.29 cm. (Agriculture handbook no. 311)
          $0.70

          1.Interest and usury-Tables, etc. 2.Forests and
       forestry-Tables and ready-reckoners.  I. Neebe,
       David J., 1929- joint author, II. Title, Series:
       U.S. Dept. of Agriculture handbook, no. 311)

          SD393.M33              511.8           Agr66-242
```

Title card, entered by title of book

```
SD
143    National Association of State Foresters
N3          Forests and forestry in the American States; a
       reference anthology. Ralph R. Widner, editor.
       [Missoula, Mont., 1968]
          xx, 594 p. illus., map (on lining paper),
       ports.  23 cm.


          1.Forests and forestry-U.S.-Addresses, essays,
       lectures. 2.Forest protection-Law and legisla-
       tion-Addresses, essays, lectures. 3.Forest man-
       agement-Addresses, essays, lectures.  I. Widner,
       Ralph R., ed.  II.Title.
       SD143.N3              ◯  634.9´0973      68-27166
       Library of Congress    [69f5]
```

**Corporate author card, entered by society, institution,
government, or other group responsible for authorship of the book**

```
QC
983    U.S. *Weather Bureau*
U58cn       Climatological data; national summary. v.1-
       Jan. 1950-
       [v.p.]
             v. maps. 28 cm. monthly.
       Each vol. includes an annual issue.



          1.U.S.-Climate. 2.Meteorology-U.S.  I.Title.
       QC983.A535                              55-58495
                               ◯
       Library of Congress  [60b¼]
```

Corporate author card showing a government agency as author

Filing Rules

To standardize access to information, all libraries using the Library of Congress classification system adhere to similar rules for filing and cataloging. Remember, however, that even standardized rules change periodically, and you may notice variations. The following are a few representative rules.

1. Cards are arranged alphabetically, with words rather than letters as units: *word-by-word* alphabetizing.
   Example: *New York* precedes *Newark*

2. Articles at the beginning of the title are ignored, but they are considered when in the middle of the title.
   Example: *A Man and a Woman* is filed as *Man and a Woman*
   BUT
   Man and Environment precedes *Man and the Environment*

3. Numbers in titles are spelled out as words, and in the language of the rest of the title.
   Example: *100 Trees* is filed as *One Hundred Trees*
   100 Jahre is filed as *Hundert Jahre*

4. Plain initials are filed at the beginning of a letter.
   Example: *FAO* (abbreviation for "Food and Agriculture Organization") is filed at the beginning of the F's
   But acronyms are filed as if they were actual words.
   Example: *FORTRAN* follows *forest*

5. Exact spelling of author's name or book title is always followed.
   Example: Hoffman   Encyclopaedia
   Hoffmann   Encyclopedia
   Hofman

6. Names with a "von" and "de la" may be found in one of several places, depending upon the country of origin.
   Example: Butler, Harro von
   Elner von Eschenback, Marie
   Von Braun, Werner
   De la More, Maria
   La Bruyere, Jean de
   Paz, Luciana de la

7. Names beginning with Mc are usually filed as though they started with Mac.
   Example· Mac Bein
   McElroy
   Machine
   Mackintosh
   McLoud

8. Some abbreviations, such as U.S., are filed as if they were spelled out.

Evaluating Material

As you locate books on the shelves, critically examine each one for its relevance to your topic. Make a brief note on your bibliographic card to indicate the book's significance, if any. This preliminary examination of a book could include the following steps.

1. Examine the title page.
   a. Note the title and subtitle. Frequently the subtitle gives that extra piece of information that identifies the tone of the work—e.g., *Multiple Purpose River Development: Studies in Applied Economic Analysis.*
   b. Note the author's qualifications. Is he a specialist in the field? Look askance at a sociologist (even with a Ph.D.) writing on polymers. Don't rely on the book jacket alone for the author's credentials. The jacket may overstate the author's qualifications because one of its purposes is to sell the book. If in doubt, check the author's credentials in a reputable biographical source (e.g., *American Men and Women of Science*]. Note the author's academic or professional affiliation.
   c. Note the publisher. Some publishers are more likely to publish scholarly books than others: for example, university presses usually publish scholarly works. Examples of some of the more well-known science publishers are:
      Academic   McGraw-Hill
      Pergamon   Prentice-Hall
      Wiley   Williams & Wilkins
   d. Note the date of publication. Was the book written recently enough to be helpful? In scientific literature the more current literature is usually looked at first. However, much depends on the subject. An 1870 botany book can be entirely relevant today but a ten-year-old engineering book can be too old. The time lag between publication date and the actual research can be anywhere from five to ten years. Therefore, as a rule, the more current the publication date, the better.
   e. Note the copyright date. A copyright is granted by the United States government to writers of original works and it protects their writings from being copied without permission. The date can usually be found on the back of the title page and may give a better indication of the age of the information than the date of publication.
2. Examine the table of contents. Chapter titles and major divisions of the book will give you an idea of the broad subjects covered.
3. Examine the preface. This frequently overlooked or ignored part of the book often indicates the scope of coverage, the audience written for, the treatment of subject, or special features and limitations.
4. Look for an index. The index gives an alphabetical listing of the names, ideas, and small topics discussed in the book and tells where to find them. Check the index to see which aspects of your topic are covered.

Additional Sources to Check

You may want to find books on your topic that are not in the library you are using. Examples of sources to use for this type of search follow.

Books in Print (BIP): This source is a listing of books presently available from most major U.S. publishers. It is organized in three volumes: author, title, and subject. Other information within the entries includes the price, publisher, and data of publication. The same publisher also issues *Paperbound Books in Print* and *Forthcoming Books.*

Cumulative Book Index (CBI): this is an author, title, subject index to current books published internationally in the English language. Excluded from *CBI* are pamphlets and government documents. Entries are in alphabetical order and include the following information: price, publisher, paging, edition, and date of publication. *CBI* is issued monthly (except August) and is cumulated annually.

Library of Congress, Books, Subject: This is a book version of the subject card catalog of the Library of Congress. Consequently, the LC subject headings on your search term list can be used when searching this source. Numerous cumulations are available.

National Agricultural Library Catalog: This multivolume book version of the card catalog at the National Agricultural Library includes books, periodicals, and serials and can be searched by author, title, or subject. It has been issued in two major sets: 1862-1965 and 1966-1970. Each set includes cards for publications received and catalogued, *not* published, between the dates indicated. Since 1970 it has been issued monthly and indexed annually.

Department of the Interior, Dictionary Catalog of the Department Library: This book version of the card catalog at the Department of Interior library represents one of the largest specialized collections in the United States of materials on natural resources, conservation, and reclamation. It includes all forms of publications (books, periodicals, government documents, etc.) which can be searched by title, author, or subject. The first set of volumes includes material catalogued before December 1965. The supplements cover additions to the catalog.

Dictionary Catalog of the Yale Forestry Library: This book version of the card catalog at the Yale Forestry School Library includes over 90,000 volumes received before 1962. All types of publications are catalogued, including more than 38,000 cards representing periodical articles from several major forestry journals. The catalog can be searched using authors, titles, or subjects.

Catalog of the Conservation Library Denver Public Library, 1974- : This book catalog of materials from the Conservation Library of the Denver Public Library covers the field of environment from various aspects. Economic, social, historical, and management material is available, as well as materials on the broad aspects of the conservation movement. The accent is on the environmental aspects, not the technical. This catalog can be searched by author, title, and subject.

Retrieving Books—A Strategy

1. Search the shelves to find the books identified in the card catalog.
2. Search the shelf area around the location of relevant books. This shelf search is one way of making the LC classification scheme work for you. Note any relevant materials not found in the previous catalog search. List these books by author and title. If a shelf list is available, use it instead of the shelf search.
3. Look up any new books in the author/title catalog. What tracings do these

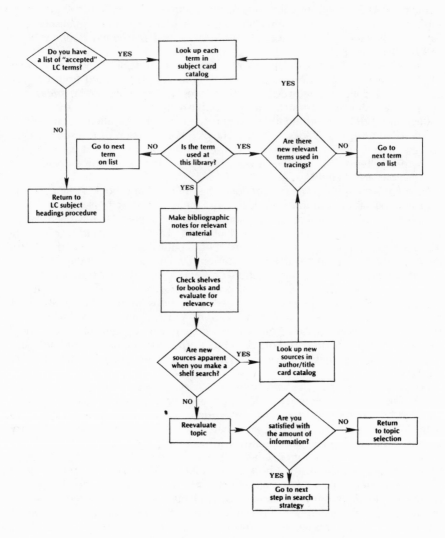

Figure 6. Retrieving books—flowchart

new books have? Any new tracings should be added to your search term list.

4. Using these new terms, repeat the process (subject catalog, shelf, author/title catalog, search), adding any new and relevant material to your growing bibliography.

5. Continue to repeat the process until a pattern emerges and no more new material is added to the bibliography.

6. Using the most frequently encountered Library of Congress call numbers noted in this process, do a shelf search in other locations (e.g., in the reference collection, oversize book shelves, other libraries).

7. Search *BIP, CBI, LC* catalog, and other libraries' book catalogs for additional material.

8. Record new search terms in your research log.

9. Add any new information to your bibliographic note cards.

10. Note in your research log the sources you searched and the steps you took.

11. Evaluate your topic. If you are finding too much material, consider limiting your topic. In any case, take any steps necessary to modify your original topic. A good researcher must be continually attuned to changes or new or new avenues in his topic. When interesting side roads appear, note them. These are frequently the best sources for future research topics.

Chapter 6

Indexes and Abstracts

This chapter will answer these key questions:

1. What are indexes and abstracts?
2. How are appropriate indexes and abstracts identified?
3. What criteria can be used when you examine an index or abstract?
4. What role can a computer play in a literature search?
5. What is a current awareness service and how can it help?
6. What is a good strategy to follow when searching indexes and abstracts?

A library catalog may be the major index to a library's collection, but its usefulness is limited when you are trying to locate specific articles in periodicals and other serials. You may use a catalog to determine if the library *has* a particular serial or journal, but the catalog will not indicate what articles appear within *specific* issues of the serial. The key to serial and journal literature is indexes and abstracts.

Indexes and Abstracts

In simplest terms, an index is a list—for example, a list of all subjects treated in a book with the page numbers on which they are discussed. This chapter will focus on indexing services which either index the literature of a field of study or the information from a given set of journals. Enough bibliographic information is included in the index citation for you to retrieve the original source. Indexes can be arranged in a number of ways—for example, by author, title, subject, institution, or species—or any combination of these. Almost all use some sort of alphabetical arrangement.

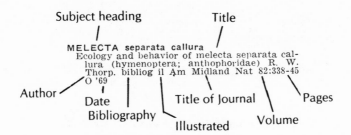

Sample index citation

43

An *abstract* includes not only the bibliographic information necessary to retrieve the original article but also a summary—or abstract—of the material being indexed. Abstract publications are sometimes referred to as "abstracting journals" or "abstracting services."

The abstracts in an abstracting journal may be listed alphabetically or arranged in broad subject categories. One or more indexes are usually included to help locate the abstracts and the index entry includes a location symbol (a page or abstract number, for example). Some types of indexes that might be found in an abstracting service include:

1. *An author index,* or list of all the authors (including joint authors) of articles included in that issue of the abstract.
2. *A subject index,* or list of all abstracts that deal with a particular subject listed under that subject heading.
3. *A geographic index,* or list of references to all abstracts that relate to a particular geographic area.
4. *A species index,* or list of all abstracts that deal with a particular species.

An abstracting service, if available, is usually more helpful than an index. You can better determine whether or not to retrieve the material after reading the abstract (as opposed to reading just the title in an index citation). Also, because most abstracting services include one or more indexes, your chances of finding an appropriate article are increased.

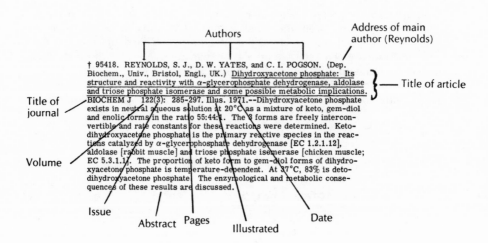

Sample entry from an abstract journal

Identifying Appropriate Indexes and Abstracts

Each index or abstracting service has a unique approach to the literature and therefore differs from all others in both scope and general subject coverage. When searching for serial or journal literature on a particular topic, it is important to be able to identify the indexes and abstracts which are most appropriate to your subject. There are a number of ways to do this.

For example, a guide to the literature in a particular field will list the indexes and abstracts relevant to that field. There are also general source guides to the literature that recommend sources by field of study. Two such general guides to the literature are Eugene P. Sheehy, *Guide to Reference Books,* and A.J. Walford, *Guide to Reference Material.* A more complete description of this type of source is included in Chapter 8, "Reference Materials."

Another method of identifying these sources is to search the subject catalog. At the time your were searching the catalog for monographs you might have noted a relevant index source. Because most indexes have such broad coverage, they also have entries in the subject catalog under broad headings with the subdivision *"ABSTRACTS."*

There are directories to periodicals that give bibliographic and editorial information about periodicals. Frequently these sources include information about where a certain journal or group of journals is indexed or abstracted. A well-known source that can be used to locate this type of information is *Ulrich's International Periodical Directory.* Ulrich's lists periodicals by broad subject areas and is helpful for locating the major journals in a field. For example, there are 180 journals listed for the field of *forestry* alone. However, journals are also listed under forestry-related terms, such as *lumber* and *con-servation.* Each journal citation gives complete bibliographic and editorial information.

A periodical or serial may publish its own index. However, using these indexes eliminates the chance of locating relevant articles in other journals.

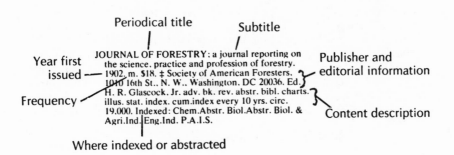

Sample entry from Ulrich's

These indexes are best used when you *know* an article appeared in a particular journal but you can't remember *when* it appeared.

And don't forget that in this area, too, one of your best sources for guidance and help is your reference librarian.

Using Indexes and Abstracts

Numerous indexes and abstracts are important to anyone searching topics within the environmental sciences. Each source is different in terms of what it covers, how it is arranged, and, consequently, how it is used. Because of the uniqueness of each of these sources it is difficult to describe all indexes and abstracts together, and to recommend a single method for searching.

It is helpful, however, to examine each possible new source and to discover as much as you can about it *before* you try to use it. The following is a checklist of some important questions you should ask about each new index or abstract you use. Not all questions will apply to all sources.

Checklist of Questions to Answer about
Indexing and Abstracting Services

1. What specific subject areas are covered?
2. Does the index or abstract publication include instructions for using it?
3. Is there a list of the specific primary sources indexed or abstracted?
4. Is there a list of abbreviations used?
5. Is there a list or thesaurus of the terms (subject headings or key words) used by the index or abstract?
6. How often is the index or abstract issued?
7. Are there cumulations? (A cumulated index consolidates monthly or yearly indexes into one alphabetical sequence. Thus a researcher can consult one source for information rather than, say, 12 monthly issues or 5 yearly issues.)
8. If an index, how are the citations entered? By author? Title? Subject? Other?
9. If an abstracting journal, how are the abstracts arranged? In a classified order? Alphabetical order? By accession number? Other?
10. If an abstracting journal, what type of indexes are included, if any? Author? Title? Subject? Geographic? Corporate? Species? Other?
11. What types of material are indexed or abstracted? Journal articles? Books? Government publications? Proceedings? Other?
12. What is the language of the material covered? English only? Foreign languages?
13. Is the material covered technical and research-oriented or popular? Or both?
14. Are there any other special or unique features?

The appendix of this book includes a selected list of indexes and abstracts in which the scope and coverage of major sources for searching the literature of the environmental sciences are described. Before using these tools in your literature search, examine each thoroughly according to the preceding checklist. You may want to include a checklist for each relevant source in your research log.

Examining each index and abstract according to the checklist should familiarize you with the source. However, applying a checklist alone may not teach you the actual use of a particular tool. Once you become familiar with an index or abstract, try to search your topic. This gives you the opportunity to learn by doing. If at any point something is not clear, even after careful examination and practice, ask a reference librarian to help you.

Examples of Checklist Applied to Some Major Sources

The following examples show how the checklist can be applied to some of the major sources used in searching the literature of the environmental sciences.

Biological Abstracts

Specific subject areas covered? The cover lists these subject areas:

Aerospace Biology	Microbiology
Agriculture	Nutrition
Bacteriology	Parasitology
Behavioral Sciences	Pathology—animal and plant
Biochemistry	Pharmacology
Bioinstrumentation	Physiology—animal and plant
Biophysics	Public Health
Cell Biology	Radiation Biology
Environmental Biology	Systematic Biology
Experimental Medicine	Toxicology
Genetics	Veterinary Science
Immunology	Virology

User instructions? As of 1977 each issue includes a foldout page at the back of the issue titled "Guidelines for Searching Biological Abstracts and Bioresearch Index." Previously, separately published guides to *Biological Abstracts* were available. Instructions for each index are included with each index.

List of primary sources indexed? A separate annual publication, *BIOSIS List of Serials,* lists the primary sources covered by BIOSIS, including title abbreviations, and new, changed, or ceased titles.

List of abbreviations? The January and July issues (No. 1 of a new volume) contain a list of abbreviations and symbols used in abstracts. Each issue also includes "Explanations of Abbreviations Used in Biosystematic and Generic Indexes" before these two indexes.

Thesaurus of terms? Not necessary with the permuted format.

How often issued? Issued semimonthly.

Cumulations? Cumulated semiannually.

Arrangement? Abstracts are numbered consecutively and arranged under detailed subject categories as outlined in the subject guide at the beginning of each issue. Subject, author, biosystematic, generic, and concept indexes appear in each issue and are cumulated semiannually.

Type of material covered? Biological Abstracts covers books, letters (very few), notes (very few), and primarily research journals and serials. Its companion tool, *Bioresearch Index,* covers annual reports, bibliographies, book chapters, data reports, nomenclature rules, notes, review journals, research journals, symposium abstracts, and symposium papers.

Language of Material? Covers English and foreign language materials.

Technical and/or popular material? Technical and research-oriented.

Special features? Each issue includes a section titled "New Books Received." New journals received are listed under the heading "General Biology."

Biological and Agricultural Index

Specific subject areas covered? The introduction list these subject areas:

Agricultural Chemicals	Forestry
Agricultural Economics	Genetics
Agricultural Engineering	Horticulture
Agriculture and Agricultural Research	Marine Biology
Animal Husbandry	Microbiology
Bacteriology	Mycology
Biochemistry	Nutrition
Biology	Pesticides
Botany	Physiology
Conservation	Poultry
Dairying and Dairy Products	Soil Science
Ecology	Veterinary Medicine
Entomology	Virology
Food Science	Zoology

User instructions? Each issue includes a sample entry with an accompanying explanation in the preliminary pages, as does the annual cumulative volume.

List of primary sources indexed? Each annual cumulative volume includes a list of periodicals indexed.

List of abbreviations? Each issue includes a list of abbreviations of periodicals indexed as well as a separate listing of other abbreviations used.

Thesaurus of terms? No, but subject headings are typed in bold print.

How often issued? Issued monthly (except August).

Cumulations? Cumulated annually.

Arrangement? Entries are arranged by subject in an alphabetical listing.

Type of material covered? Periodicals only.

Language of material? English language materials only.

Technical and/or popular materials? Primarily technical and research-oriented but also covers some popular material.

Special features? Each issue contains an author listing of citations to book reviews.

Chemical Abstracts

Specific subject areas covered? Preliminary pages list these subject areas:

Biochemistry
Organic Chemistry

Macromolecular Chemistry
Applied Chemistry and Chemical Engineering
Physical and Analytical Chemistry

User instructions? An illustrative key to *Chemical Abstracts,* a brief guide to its use, is found in the first issue of a volume. In addition an *Index Guide* and *Index Guide Supplement* are published separately. Together these provide a user with cross-references, synonyms, indexing policy notes, and instructions for the use of Chemical Abstracts Service products.

List of primary sources indexed? CASSI—*Chemical Abstract Service Source Index*—list the abbreviations used and indicates where sources may be found.

List of abbreviations? The first issue of a volume includes a list of abbreviations and symbols used.

Thesaurus of terms? A separately published *Index Guide* lists index terms and names to be used in searching the volume indexes of *Chemical Abstracts.*

How often issued? Issued weekly.

Cumulations? Indexes cumulated semiannually.

Arrangement? Abstracts are numbered and classified according to subject. They are arranged within 80 subject groups. Within each group, journals, proceedings, edited collections, technical reports, and dissertation abstracts precede new book announcements which in turn precede patent abstracts. A keyword index, author index, numerical patent index, and patent concordance are included in each issue. Chemical Substance Index, General Subject Index, Formula Index, Index of Ring Systems, Author Index, Numerical Patent Index, and Patent Concordance are volume indexes.

Type of material covered? Journals, patents, reviews, technical reports, monographs, conference proceedings, symposia, dissertations, and books.

Language of material? English and foreign language materials.

Technical and/or popular materials? Technical and research-oriented.

Environment Abstracts

Specific subject areas covered? Twenty-one subject categories as outlined in the table of contents are:

Air Pollution
Chemical and Biological Contamination
Energy
Environmental Education
Environmental Design and Urban Ecology
Food and Drugs
General
International
Land Use and Misuse
Noise Pollution
Non-Renewable Resources
Oceans and Estuaries
Population Planning and Control
Radiological Contamination
Renewable Resources—Terrestrial

Renewable Resources—Water
Solid Waste
Transportation
Water Pollution
Weather Modification and Geophysical Change
Wildlife

User instructions? Each issue contains a section "How to Use Environment Abstracts" in its introductory pages.

List of primary sources indexed? At the back of each issue is a periodicals list of those publications searched regularly for environmental information. The list does not include the reports, government documents, conference proceedings, etc., also covered by the service.

List of abbreviations? Each issue lists abbreviations on the inside of the back cover.

Thesaurus of terms? Yes. *Environment Index*—the annual cumulation—contains a section "Subject Terms: Keyword List" as well as "SIC Code Terms: Keyword List."

How often issued? Issued monthly (bimonthly July-August). Issued bimonthly before 1974.

Cumulations? Cumulative indexes are in the annually cumulated *Environment Index*: subject, Standard Industrial Code, geography, Federal Register, author.

Arrangement? Abstracts are numbered consecutively and arranged under the 21 subject categories. Subject, industry (SIC codes), and author are included in each issue. *Environment Index* serves as a yearbook and as the cumulative annual index to the monthly issues of *Environment Abstracts*.

Type of material covered? Periodicals/journals, special reports, government documents, conference proceedings, irregular serials, speeches, newsletters, hearings, monographs, statistics, newspapers, and films.

Language of material? English and foreign language materials covered.

Technical and/or popular material? Technical and nontechnical coverage.

Special features? Each issue has these special sections: (a) "Issue Alert" a guide to significant information appearing in the issue; (b) "Federal Register," a guide to significant environmental entries from this record; (c) "Conferences," a list of conferences of interest; and (d) "New Books in Print."

Forestry Abstracts

Specific subject areas covered? Areas covered as outlined in the table of contents are:

General
Factors of the Environment. Biology
Silviculture
Work Study. Harvesting of Wood: Logging and Transport. Forest
    Engineering
Forest Injuries and Protection
Forest Mensuration. Increment; Development and Structure of Stands.
    Surveying and Mapping Organization of Forest Enterprises

Marketing of Forest Products. Economics of Forest Transport and the Wood Industries.

Forest Products and Their Utilization

Forests and Forestry From the National Point of View. Social Economics of Forestry

User instructions? The beginning of each issue includes brief instructions in the section titled "Readers' Guide."

List of abbreviations? The beginning of each issue lists abbreviations in the section titled "Readers' Guide."

Thesaurus of terms? No.

How often issued? Issued monthly (quarterly before 1973).

Cumulations? Indexes cumulated annually.

Arrangement? Abstracts are numbered consecutively and arranged according to the Oxford System of Decimal Classification for Forestry, as outlined in the beginning of each issue. Author and species index in each issue. Cumulative annual indexes include author, species, and subject.

Type of material covered? Journals, government publications, serials, and books.

Language of material? English and foreign language materials covered.

Technical and/or popular material? Primarily technical and research-oriented.

Monthly Catalog of U.S. Government Publications

Specific subject areas covered? Many topics are covered. All publications are issued from branches of the U.S. government and thus would reflect the issues of concern to those bodies.

User instructions? The beginning of each issue includes instructions in the section titled "Users' Guide."

List of primary sources indexed? No.

List of abbreviations? The beginning of each issue lists abbreviations in the section titled "Users' Guide."

Thesaurus of terms? No.

How often issued? Issued monthly.

Cumulations? Indexes cumulated semiannually and annually.

Arrangement? Each entry is numbered and arranged under the issuing agency. Issuing agencies are arranged alphabetically. Author, title, subject, and series/report indexes appear in each issue.

Type of material covered? Government publications issued by all branches of the U.S. government.

Language of material? English only.

Technical and/or popular material? Material covered includes both technical and popular publications.

New York Times Index

Specific subject areas covered? The *New York Times Index* is an index to news and editorial material as recorded in the late city edition of *The New York Times.* Thus its subject coverage is varied and broad.

User instructions? Each issue includes instructions on use of the index, following the index portion. Annual cumulative volumes include the instructions in the preliminary pages.

List of primary sources indexed? Yes. The late city edition of *The New York Times*.

List of abbreviations? Each issue contains a "Key to Abbreviations" following the instructions on the use of the index. Annual cumulative volumes include the list of abbreviations in the preliminary pages of the one-volume indexes or at the beginning of the second volume in a two-volume annual index.

Thesaurus of terms? Yes. *The New York Times Thesaurus of Descriptors,* a separate publication.

How often issued? Issued semimonthly.

Cumulations? Cumulated annually.

Arrangement? Abstracts of news and editorial matter are arranged under headings and their subdivisions, which are arranged alphabetically. Under a heading, entries are arranged chronologically.

Type of material covered? News and editorial matter of *The New York Times.* The index also covers the Sunday supplements (*Book Review* and *Magazine*) as well as advertisements that are related to the news and are of interest to users.

Language of material? English language only.

Special features? Certain semimonthly issues contain a section titled "New York Times Index Highlights," a section of citations from *The New York Times,* which cover a stated period and are centered on a given topic. The "Highlights" form a series of topically focused bibliographies drawn from *The New York Times.*

Science Citation Index

Science Citation Index is an example of a citation index. These indexes take advantage of the proven concept that authors' references (citations) to previously published material indicate subject relationships between current articles and older publications. In addition, articles that refer to (cite) the same publications usually have subject relationships with each other.

Applying these relationships, the citation indexes show, for the period covered, which previously published items are being referred to (cited) in the current literature, who is doing the citing, and in what journals they are being cited.

Specific subject areas covered? The subtitle describes the categories that are covered: "An international interdisciplinary index to the literature of science, medicine, agriculture, technology and the behavioral sciences."

User instructions? Directions for use of the *complete* index are printed in a separate guide, published annually. Instructions for the use of each specific index (*Source Index, Citation Index*) are printed on the front and back covers of each volume.

List of primary sources indexed? Yes. A list of primary sources covered by the service is in the separate *Science Citation Index Guide and Journal Lists,* published annually, as well as in the annual *Source Index.*

List of abbreviations? Abbreviations are listed in the *Science Citation Index*

Guide, a separate publication. Each volume also includes a list in preliminary pages.

Thesaurus of terms? None is required with a permuterm subject index.

How often issued? Issued quarterly and annually.

Cumulations? Cumulated annually. Five-year cumulation (1965-1969).

Arrangement? (a) In the *Citation Index* entries are arranged alphabetically by cited author and, within this, chronologically by cited year. (b) In the Source *Index* entries are arranged alphabetically by author. (c) In the *Patent Citation Index* entries are arranged in numerical order by patent number. (d) In the *Corporate Index* entries are arranged alphabetically by organization. (e) In the *Permuterm Subject Index* entries are arranged alphabetically by subject term.

Type of material covered? Journals.

Language of material? English and foreign language materials covered.

Technical and/or popular materials? Primarily technical and research-oriented.

Sociological Abstracts

Specific subject areas covered? The table of contents lists these areas:

Methodology and Research Technology
Sociology: History and Theory
Social Psychology
Group Interactions
Culture and Social Structure
Complex Organizations (Management)
Social Change and Economic Development
Mass Phenomena
Political Interactions
Social Differentiation
Rural Sociology and Agricultural Economics
Urban Structures and Ecology
Sociology of the Arts
Sociology of Education
Sociology of Religion
Social Control
Sociology of Science
Demography and Human Biology
The Family and Socialization
Sociology and Health and Medicine
Social Problems and Social Welfare
Sociology and Knowledge
Community Development
Policy Planning, Forecasting and Speculation
Radical Sociology
Environmental Interactions
Studies in Poverty
Studies in Violence
Feminist Studies

User Instructions? No.

List of primary sources indexed? Yes. Listed in the periodicals index in each issue.

List of abbreviations? A list of abbreviations is included on the inside of the back cover of each issue.

Thesaurus of terms? No.

How often issued? Issued five times annually.

Cumulations? Cumulated annually.

Arrangement? Abstracts are numbered and arranged by subject as outlined in the table of contents. Author, subject, and periodical indexes are in each issue.

Type of material covered? Journals.

Language of material? English and foreign language materials covered.

Technical and/or popular material? Primarily technical and research-oriented.

Special features? Some issues include supplements with abstracts of conference papers.

Computerized Searches and Current Awareness Services

Computers are having a profound influence on the information process. Many of the indexes and abstracts you learn about in this chapter are now, or will soon be, available in computer-searchable form. While a thorough manual search can take days or weeks, a computerized search can usually be done in a matter of hours or even minutes. The product of a computerized search is a printout of all relevant citations from the data base. These citations are sometimes accompanied by abstracts. Many libraries now have these computerized searches available, and although there is sometimes a charge, it is usually nominal when compared to the labor cost of a manual search. Examples of computerized data bases and their printed counterparts are shown below.

Data Base	Printed Index
CA Condensates	*Chemical Abstracts*
MEDLARS	*Index Medicus*
Psychological Abstracts	*Psychological Abstracts*
Compendex	*Engineering Index*
BIOSIS Previews	*Biological Abstracts* and *Bioresearch Index*
ERIC	*Research in Education* and *Current Index to Journals in Education*
Pollution Abstracts	*Pollution Abstracts*
ENVIROLINE	Covers all Environment Information Center publications
ENVIROBIB	*Environmental Periodical Bibliography*
AGRICOLA (formerly CAIN)	National Agricultural Library Catalog and Index
SCISEARCH	*Science Citation Index*
NTIS	*Government Reports Announcements and Index*

Many commercial companies are being formed that deal specifically with the computerized aspect of the information process. These companies provide a variety of services, including the following:

1. *Comprehensive searches.* For a fee, these services search through every data bank available to them for all relevant information on your topic.
2. *Current awareness services.* These services periodically scan their data banks for the newest information on your topic. This update of information will be sent to you on a regular basis (e.g., weekly or monthly).
3. *Published current awareness services.* Many companies prepare weekly current awareness publications on high-interest areas. An example of this type of publications is *Current Contents,* a weekly publication that reprints the tables of contents of important journals. It is published by the Institute for Scientific Information and is available in six different editions as follows: (1) Life Sciences, (2) Clinical Practice, (3) Agriculture, Biology, and Environmental Science, (4) Physical and Chemical Sciences, (5) Behavioral, Social and Educational Sciences, and (6) Engineering and Technology.

While the cost of these searches and services may at first sound prohibitive, the advantages usually outweigh the expense. Many professionals do not have the time to regularly search their professional literature, and computerized searches or current awareness services save money by saving labor cost.

Another advantage to these services is that they can supply you with information when you don't have a library. For example, if you are doing research in a remote location, a current awareness service could help you keep up with the literature.

Indexes and Abstracts Search Strategy

1. State the object of your search in a sentence of brief paragraph. Write this in your reserach log. If necessary, modify the statement you made when you clarified your topic in Chapter 3.
2. List all the key words or search terms in your research log. Remember to add those terms you have used in Chapters 3 and 4. Use a dictionary to add any synonyms.
3. Add to this list as appropriate:
   a. Subdivisions of the topic
   b. Names of researches in the field
   c. Institutions doing work in the field
   d. Genus species
   e. Trade names
4. Set the parameters of your search. If it is a taxonomical search, it will require an extensive retrospective search. For new fields, probably all the important references will be found within the last few years.
5. Identify the appropriate indexes and abstracts for your topic. List them in your research log.
6. Study each source according to the checklist in this chapter. Keep these notes in your log.

7. Note whether your search terms are used. If they are not, what terms relevant to your search are used?
8. Watch for changes as you search. Terminology can change from one year to the next. Indexes and abstracts may change their format or scope.

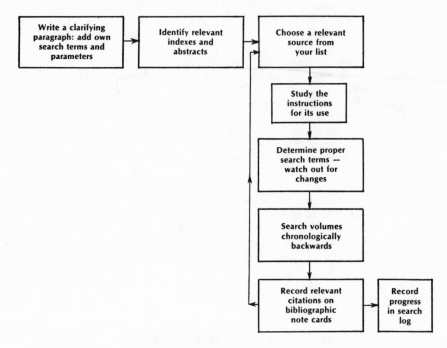

Figure 7. Index and abstract search strategy flowchart

9. Look for cumulated issues which allow you to do a comprehensive search.
10. Search backwards chronologically in each index and abstract. You might find a reference for a bibliography in .a 1972 index that covers the literature for 1965-1971. This could save many hours of searching time.
11. When relevant citations are located, record each one on bibliographic note cards. Follow the same guidelines that were outlined for bibliographic cards in Chapter 4.
12. Because mistakes can happen, keep track of where you find each citation. A simple code on your bibliographic card is sufficient. For Example: *Environ. Per. Bib.* vol 3: 12366 (1974). This could be located on the bibliographic card. It means the citation was found in *Environmental Periodicals Bibliography,* vol. 3 (1974), abstract number 12366.
13. Always keep track of your progress during any one working session. You don't want to cover the same material twice, so keep a running

```
┌─────────────────────────────────────────────┬──────────────────┐
│ McINTOSH, A.W. & N.R. KEVERN                  │ Call Number      │
│ Author                                        │ and Source       │
│ TOXICITY OF COPPER TO ZOOPLANKTON             │ J547             │
│ Title                                         │ ENVIRON. PER.BM  │
│ J. OF ENVIRONMENTAL QUALITY                   │ VOL.3: 123-66    │
│ Serial or Periodical                          │    (1974)        │
├───────────────────────────────────────────────────────────────┤
│ City        Publisher                                           │
│ 1974        3(NO.2) AP/JUNE        166                          │
│ Year        Volume        Pages                                 │
│ REPORT OF SPECIFIC STUDY, CHARTS, TABLES,                      │
│ Remarks      GOOD  BIBLIOGRAPHY.                                │
└───────────────────────────────────────────────────────────────┘
```

Bibliographic note for serial

record of what volumes you have searched in which index or abstract. Include it in your research log. A sample of this record follows the flowchart at the end of this chapter.

14. Reevaluate your topic once again. You may want to modify your strategy. Are you finding too much material? Have you read something that lends a different slant to the search?

15. Continue to add and delete search terms. Watch for variations in terms and spelling as you move from one index to another. Example: One index might use WOOD LOTS; another WOODLOTS. These two spellings can be pages or volumes apart, so don't overlook them. Be aware also that every index will probably have a different approach to your topic. This difference will show up in the terminology used in the subject index. Example: FORESTRY—MANAGEMENT or MANAGEMENT—FORESTRY.

16. Remember that there is a time lag from when an article is written to when it is cited in an index. For this reason remember to use current awareness services to bring you up to date. You might also consider searching current issues of those periodicals which, as a result of your index and abstract searches, you have identified as being pertinent to your topic.

17. Inquire about the availability of computer searches for your topic and consider the advantages of using one.

At this point in your search a research log is especially important. The preceding strategy suggests several ways you can be using a log when you search indexes and abstracts. Following the steps of this strategy and carefully recording each step in your log should ensure that your search is orderly and thorough.

TITLE: Irrigation and its effects on growing apples   DATE: April 7, 1977   PAGE: 1

SOURCE	SUBJECT	VOLUME	DATE	NOTES
Biological and Agricultural Index	Irrigation	29 28 27 26	'74-'75 '73-'74 '72-'73 '71-'72	Searched all cross-headings under irrigation and other terms beginning with "irrigation."
Biological and Agricultural Index	Orchard irrigation	29 28 27 26	'74-'75 '73-'74 '72-'73 '71-'72	
Biological and Agricultural Index	Apples - field research	29 28 27	'74-'75 '73-'74 '72-'73	Stopped searching at 1972. No results with this heading.
Bibliography of Agriculture	Irrigation	29	'75	Searched key words "apples" and "fruit."

Literature search record

Chapter 7

Locating Serials

This chapter will answer these key questions:

1. How can serial abbreviations be deciphered?
2. How are specific serials located in the library?
3. How can serial literature be evaluated?
4. What are some methods of taking notes on serial literature?
5. How are government publications located?
6. What is a union list and how does it help in the location of serial titles?
7. What is interlibrary loan and how is this service used?

Once you have identified relevant citations in indexes and abstracts you will want to retrieve and examine the original articles. This gathering process can involve a number of steps and a careful strategy is important.

Deciphering Serial Abbreviations

The first step in gathering serials is to be sure you have a complete and accurate citation. Checking through your bibliographic note cards you may notice that many or most of the periodical and serial citations are abbreviated. Interpreting this abbreviation is sometimes difficult.

To decipher serial abbreviations, first return to the source where you found the abbreviation and look for a list of abbreviations used. Most indexes and abstracts have such a list; sometimes they are published in a separate volume. Some examples of these tools include:

Chemical Abstracts Services Source Index (CASSI), 1907-1974 with quarterly supplements, Chemical Abstracts Service, Columbus, Ohio. This source provides a key to the abbreviations used in *Chemical Abstracts*.

BIOSIS; List of Serials with Coden, Title Abbreviations, New Changed and Ceased Titles, annual, Biosciences Information Service of Biological Abstracts, Philadelphia. This source provides a key to the abbreviations used in *Biological Abstracts*.

Publications Indexed for Engineering (PIE), annual, Engineering Index, Inc., New York. This source provides a key to the abbreviations used in *Engineering Index*.

Bibliographic Guide for Editors and Authors, 1974, American Chemical Society, Washington, D.C. This is a combined source list compiled from the three sources above (*CASSI, List of Serials and PIE*).

If you are still unsuccessful, ask a librarian to help you. Do not try to guess the meaning of an abbreviation.

Retrieving Serials

Once you have deciphered all your citations, continue the gathering process by determining which serials the library has. Usually serials are included in the main catalog, but sometimes you will find them in a separate file. The accompanying card samples show a variety of ways you may find serials entered in the card catalog.

Sample Card Catalog Entries
for Serials

```
Per.        Dimensions/NBS.  v.57, no.8-
D755        Aug. 1973-
            Washington, National Bureau of Standards,
            1973-

            v. monthly.

Lib. keeps  Continues Technical news bulletin.
  last 5
years only  1. Technology--Period.  I. U.S. National
            Bureau of Standards.
```

Serial entered by title

SD   United States. Northeastern Forest Experiment
11   Station, Upper Darby, Pa.
U663   U. S. D. A. Forest Service research paper NE.
            Upper Darby, Pa.
                    no. illus. 27 cm.

            Continues the Station's U.S. Forest Service
            research paper.

               1.Forests and forestry--United States--
            Collected works. I. Title.

            SD11.A455493   634.9   76-649010
            Library of Congress◯ 71 (2)

Serial entered by corporate author—a government agency

SD   New York (State) College of Forestry, Syracuse.
1   Bulletin, no. 1-6, 10-
N56   Syracuse, 1913-
                no.   in   v. illus. 23-27 cm.
            Imprint varies: Some early numbers indicate
        issuance by Syracuse University.
            1st-6th items not numbered but constitute
        no. 1-6.
            1. Forests and forestry--New York (State) 2.
        Recreation--New York (State) 3.Wood--New York
        (State) 4. Wood-using industries--New York
        (State)   ◯

Serial entry by corporate author—an institution

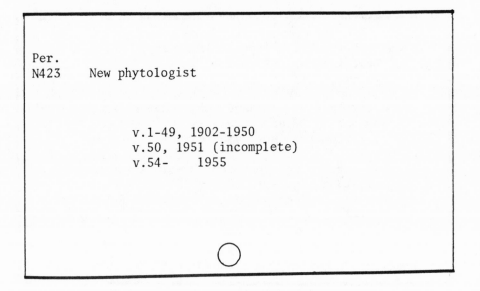

SD									
1	New York (State) College of Forestry, Syracuse.								
N56b	Bulletin, no.1-								

THOSE CHECKED ARE AVAILABLE IN LIBRARY

✓ 1	✓ 11	✓ 21	31	41	51	61	71	81	91
✓ 2	✓ 12	✓ 22	32	42	52	62	72	82	92
✓ 3	✓ 13	✓ 23	33	43	53	63	73	83	93
✓ 4	✓ 14	✓ 24	34	44	54	64	74	84	94
✓ 5	✓ 15	✓ 25	35	45	55	65	75	85	95
✓ 6	✓ 16	✓ 26	36	46	56	66	76	86	96
7	✓ 17	✓ 27	37	47	57	67	77	87	97
8	✓ 18	✓ 28	38	48	58	68	78	88	98
9	✓ 19	✓ 29	39	49	59	69	79	89	99
10	✓ 20	✓ 30	40		60	70	80	90	00

SOURCE   WHERE PUBLISHED

GIFT   PURCHASE   DOCUMENT CHECKING RECORD   DEMCO NO. 67-168

Holdings card for same serial

Per.	
N423	New phytologist
	v.1-49, 1902-1950
	v.50, 1951 (incomplete)
	v.54- 1955

Some libraries have a separate card file for
their periodical or serial holdings showing volumes owned

You may notice that these cards do not always indicate the specific volumes and dates of a serial the library owns. The information on the cards is often only editorial, telling you when the serial began publication. A holdings card may be filed behind the author or title card, indicating what specific years, issues, or volumes the library owns.

Many libraries have a computer printout of their serial collection which can be quickly updated if titles change or are added. The portability of these printouts and the ease with which they can be updated make them an invaluable source.

In some libraries different types of serials are treated differently. Frequently periodicals (a type of serial) are shelved in a separate location. If you are not sure whether the title you are looking for is considered a periodical, and possibly separate from the regular collection, ask a librarian to help you.

Serials (including periodicals) often change their name. There should be a record for any title a serial has had, as long as the library holds that title. A note on the catalog card or periodical holdings card should indicate whether that particular title is superseded, or continued by a new title, or merged with another title, as these examples indicate: *Southern Pulp and Paper Journal* SEE *Southern Pulp and Paper Manufacturer;* and *Australian Wildlife Research* supersedes *CSIRO Wildlife Research.*

As you are searching you will probably find examples of open and closed entries. An open entry is used for a work which is not complete—in other words, a work that is ongoing. An open entry indicates either when a serial began publication (e.g., V. 1— 1938—) or with which volume/number and year the library began subscribing to the serial (e.g., V. 7— 1956—).

A closed entry indicates either when the serial ceased publication or when the library stopped receiving it (e.g., V. 1—49, 1902-1950).

Some Serial Filing Rules

1. Symposia, conference proceedings, or transactions are usually entered under the name of the sponsoring agency or the title. If the words "proceedings" or "transactions" appear in the begining of the title, you may or may not find it under those words in the card catalog.

2. Serials that have a distinctive title, are entered by that title. For example, *Journal of Forestry,* a journal with a distinctive title issued by the Society of American Foresters, is filed under Journal. Some periodicals without a distinctive title, but which are issued by a society or oganization, are entered under the name of that society, for example:

    American Chemical Society. Journal
    Chemical Society, London. Journal

Once you have identified the serials you want, copy the call numbers and proceed to the stacks. Be sure you note any special location symbols.

Evaluating Serials and Taking Notes

After you have retrieved your serial articles, examine each source critically. In a preliminary examination of a journal article you should check not only title, subtitle, and author's credentials, but also the reputation of the journal itself. If the journal is one of the leaders in the field, the article is probably of high quality. Journals published by scientific organizations and educational institutions may have more prestige than trade journals because the commercial aspect is removed, but even so you should always be alert for directly or indirectly stated bias.

Taking Notes

As you examine and read articles, take careful notes. You might consider using special cards, as shown in the accompanying example.

Author's Name EMMEL, THOMAS C. Abbreviated Title (optional) ECOLOGY AND POPULATION BIOLOGY CARD #1	Keyword ECOLOGY
P. 11	"ECOLOGY IS THE SCIENTIFIC STUDY OF THE INTERRELATIONSHIPS BETWEEN ORGANISMS & THEIR ENVIRONMENT, THE PHYSICAL WORLD AROUND THEM... BEARS ON EVERY ASPECT OF OUR LIVES... VITAL TOPIC TO CONSIDER AS CURRENT POPULATION CRISIS GROWS... ENVIRONMENT IS FURTHER CHANGED BY MAN'S ACTIONS.
P. 38	THREE BASIC TYPES OF INTERSPECIFIC RELATIONS IN A BIOTIC COMMUNITY: PREDATION, SYMBIOSIS & COMPETITION
P. 39	PREDATOR - "FREE LIVING ORGANISM THAT FEEDS ON OTHER LIVING ORGANISMS, USUALLY OF ANOTHER SPECIES" (SEE NEXT CARD)

Note-taking card

Although note-taking will undoubtedly reflect your own work style, the following are suggestions for information to include:

1. Note the author's last name (and initials, if you have references to more than one author by that name).
2. If you have several articles by the same author, include an abbreviated title.
3. Note the page number or inclusive page numbers of where you found the quote or idea.
4. Try not to include more than one main quote, idea, or paraphrase per card. If more room is needed, use a second card and attach it with a clip.
5. When quoting or paraphrasing, use quotation marks and/or ellipses and *sic*.
6. At the top right, write a key word from the quote. Then, at a glance, you can tell how much information you have on each aspect of your topic. When you begin to write you can arrange these cards in outline order—in the order that the paper is to be written.
7. Complete your note-taking in one source before you go on to another.

How to Abstract

Some of your note-taking cards may include an abstract of the article or book. An abstract is a brief summary of the essential content of the original.

Abstracting the articles you read is one method of note-taking. Reading over your abstracts before you begin writing is an excellent way to review your research. When you write abstracts, keep in mind the following points:

1. Keep the abstract short but see that it contains enough information to ensure accuracy.
2. Mention the main points briefly, along with the methodology and major conclusions.
3. Use whole sentences but concise language.
4. Always read through the article once before you begin taking notes. Take notes the second time through and then condense them into your abstract.
5. Be sure to point out the uniqueness of an article. That is, what makes this article on the whitetailed deer different from all the rest?

If you have found an abstract of a significant article in one of the abstracting journals you searched, you might consider making a photocopy of it for your notes. Sometimes even making a photocopy of an entire article is faster and easier than taking extensive notes.

Retrieving Government Documents

Libraries treat government publications in a variety of ways and locating them may not be easy. Sometimes they are catalogued with the regular library collection and you will find them entered in the card catalog. In this case, keep in mind the filing rules described in Chapter 5. Watch for location symbols, as government publications could be a type of serial or may be in a special place in the library.

Many libraries are depository libraries. This means they have been designated by the U.S. government as a library in which certain government publications are deposited for the use of the public. Depository libraries often keep these documents in a separate collection and arrange them according to a special classification system (e.g., the Superintendent of Documents Classification System).

Depository libraries may have separate records (card catalogs) for their documents, or the *Monthly Catalog* may serve as an index to the library's document collection. The documents themselves may be in hard copy (books) or on microform. If it is unclear how a library handles this material, be sure to ask a librarian for help.

Because government documents are frequently kept separate from a library's main collection and may be more difficult to retrieve, they are often overlooked by library users. Yet they can be invaluable to researchers and you should try to use them.

This discussion has dealt only with publications or documents of the U.S. government. But there are other governments too—for example, New York State and Canada—which produce numerous publications. The United Nations also publishes documents. Discuss your topic with a librarian and ask if documents of states, other countries, or the United Nations might help you.

Union Lists

If your library does not have the serial you need, check a *union list* to see what other library has it. A union list includes, in alphabetical order, serials owned by a group of libraries, and the serial citation includes a list of symbols showing which libraries own the serial. Examples of union lists include:

Union List of Serials in Libraries of the United States and Canada
New Serials Titles (a supplement to the *Union List of Serials*)
New York State Union List of Serials

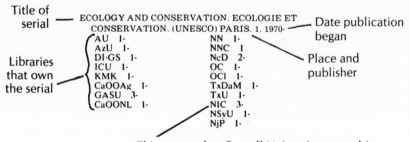

This means that Cornell University owns this serial beginning with volume 3.

Sample citation from a union list

Interlibrary Loan

When you find the library in which you are researching does not own the specific book, serial, or government publication you want, you may ask to use the services of interlibrary loan. Interlibrary loan is a cooperative arrangement which libraries throughout the country use to help their patrons obtain materials that are not available in their own libraries.

Generally, books and masters' theses can be borrowed via interlibrary loan. Very few libraries, however, will lend periodicals, reference books, rare books, or recently published books, although they may send photocopies of specific periodical articles.

The amount of time required for interlibrary loan depends on where the request is sent and how long processing takes. When you request an interlibrary loan, consider the time you have and ask the librarian if a loan seems feasible. A request could take anywhere from forty-eight hours to six months.

Each library has its own rules and policies regarding interlibrary loan. The service may be free or charges may be made for photocopying, postage, and processing. Loan periods vary, and some libraries ask that material they lend be used only in the borrowing library. There may be photoduplicating restrictions on copyrighted materials. Before you submit an ILL request, be sure you understand the rules that apply in your case. You may have explored this service when you read Chapter 2, "Library Basics."

When you submit an ILL request, be sure that you give your library a complete and accurate citation for the material you need. If possible, you should also indicate where you found the citation (i.e., the specific bibliography, abstract, or books). All this will make it easier for your loan to be processed.

Locating Serials

Retrieving the actual (primary) material you have found cited in your search of indexes and abstracts can be a complicated or involved process. A summary of the steps described in this chapter might be helpful.

1. Be sure your bibliographic cards are complete.
2. Decipher any abbreviations, using either the source of the citation or one of the tools described in this chapter.
3. Search the library's main catalog and/or whatever separate file the library uses for recording serial holdings. Be alert to some of the specific filing rules which pertain to serials.
4. Find the serials in the stacks, watching closely for location symbols. When the material is located, evaluate its relevancy and take notes.
5. Search for government documents, using the main catalog and/or separate documents catalog.
6. Locate these documents and evaluate them as you would other serials or monographs.
7. If the matarial you need is not available in your library, search union lists

to find a location, and consider using the services of interlibrary loan.

8. Throughout this process confer with a librarian whenever necessary.

9. Record your steps and progress in your research log.

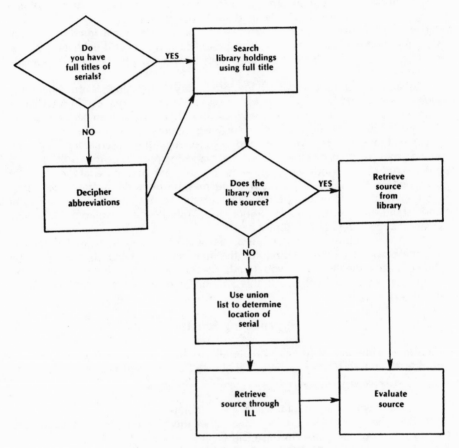

Figure 8. Locating serials — flowchart

Chapter 8
Reference Materials

This chapter will answer these key questions:

1. What are reference books?
2. What role can reference books play in a literature search?
3. What are some types of reference books?
4. How are reference books located?

A *reference book* is designed by its arrangement and treatment to be consulted for authoritative information. It is not written to be read from beginning to end. For example, sources such as the *Encyclopedia Americana* or *Webster's Dictionary* are used to locate a specific item of information or a summary discussion. Not only do we use these books in a different way from other books, but libraries frequently keep them in a separate collection.

Learning to make effective use of the reference collection is an important step in your search strategy. You used reference books such as dictionaries and encyclopedias in the initial stages of your research to help define and delimit your topic. At this point you may need additional information and reference books may again be helpful. You can use directories to find organizations or institutions doing research in your field, or consult biographical sources to determine an author's credentials, or use handbooks to gather statistics.

Complete bibliographic citations for sources mentioned in this chapter can be found at the end of the chapter.

Types of Reference Materials

Guides to the Literature

One type of reference source can help to identify other reference sources. It is called a *guide to the literature*. Such guides are compilations of titles, abstracts, indexes, bibliographies, and other major sources of a particular subject area. They try to lead a user to the major writings in a field.

All guides give slightly different information about the titles listed, and some include information on other subjects of interest to a researcher—such as how to pick a thesis topic or how to arrange personal files.

1. *General guides to the literature,* often referred to as bibliographies of bibliographies, include the major library tools of all disciplines. They can help someone approaching a subject for the first time. To locate this

type of source in the subject card catalog use subject headings like "REFERENCE BOOKS—BIBLIOGRAPHY"; "BIBLIOGRAPHY—BIBLIOGRAPHY".

Examples: E. Sheehy, *Guide to Reference Books*
A.J. Walford, *Guide to Reference Material*

These books are found in the subject catalog under the heading "REFERENCE BOOKS—BIBLIOGRAPHY."

2. *Subject guides to the literature* usually include the major tools of a particular discipline. Because their scope is narrower, subject guides can include more specific titles. They can be located in the card catalog by using the "BIBLIOGRAPHY" subheading; for example: "AGRICULTURE—BIBLIOGRAPHY," "CHEMISTRY—BIBLIOGRAPHY," or a heading such as "BIBLIOGRAPHY—BEST BOOKS—INDUSTRIAL MANAGEMENT." Subject guides can also be located by using the general (Walford and Sheehy) guides to the literature mentioned above.

Examples: In biology, Bottle, R.T. 1971, *The Use of Biological Literature* is found under "BIOLOGICAL LITERATURE" and Smith, Roger. 1972, *Guide to the Literature of the Life Sciences,* is found under "BIOLOGY—BIBLIOGRAPHY"

In chemistry, Bottle, R.T. 1969, *The Use of Chemical Literature* is found under "CHEMICAL LITERATURE"

For science in general, Lasworth, E.J. 1972, *Reference Sources in Science and Technology* is found under "SCIENCE—BIBLIOGRAPHY"

Encylopedias

An encyclopedia is usually arranged in alphabetical order, and either this and/or a detailed index allows the user to pull bits of knowledge from the set at will. There are both general and subject encyclopedias. The latter may sometimes be referred to as *cyclopedias.*

Encyclopedias are an excellent source for literature summaries. A researcher approaching a subject for the first time will find the overview provided by an encyclopedia article extremely valuable. It is a source of background information, usually including the terminology and branches of the topic. An encyclopedia may also include a bibliography at the end of each article, which can be the beginning of a collection of references on your topic.

1. *General encyclopedias* are usually listed under the subject heading "ENCYCLOPEDIAS AND DICTIONARIES."

Examples: The *Encylopeadia Britannica* and *The Encylopedia Americana* can be located under "ENCYLOPEDIAS AND DICTIONARIES."

2. *Subject encyclopedias* can be located by using the subheading "DICTIONARIES" after a subject heading; for example, "SCIENCE—DICTIONARIES"; "BOTANY—DICTIONARIES"; "BIOLOGICAL CHEMISTRY—"DICTIONARIES"; also try the subheading "COLLECTED WORKS."

Examples: *Encylcopedia of Chemical Technology* is found under "CHEM-ISTRY, TECHNICAL—DICTIONARIES"

Grzimek's Animal Life Encyclopedia is found under "ZO-OLOGY—COLLECTED WORKS"

Dictionaries

A dictionary is a book containing an alphabetical arrangement of words in a language or subject, together with their meanings or equivalents. Dictionaries are helpful for determining the meaning, pronunciation, spelling, syllabication, hyphenization, etymology, and synonyms of words. There are many types of dictionaries, such as historical, slang, usage, foreign language, synonyms and antonyms, and subject. Some of the main types of dictionaries in science libraries are the following:

1. *General English language dictionaries* include words or phrases that are English or are used by English-speaking people. Unabridged (comprehensive) dictionaries may contain much scientific terminology. Abridged (shortened) dictionaries usually include only the most commonly encountered words. Many of these dictionaries include illustrations, historical data, maps, lists of colleges and universities, etc. To locate them through the card catalog, use the subject heading "ENGLISH LANGUAGE—DICTIONARIES."
   Examples: *Webster's Third New International Dictionary of the English Language, Unabridged*

   Webster's New World Dictionary

   Both can be found in the subject card catalog under "ENGLISH LANGUAGE—DICTIONARIES"

2. *Foreign language dictionaries* are frequently bilingual, wherein the meanings of the words in one language are given in another. To locate these dictionaries, use subject headings such as "FRENCH LANGAUGE—DICTION-ARIES—ENGLISH"
   Example: *The Cambridge Italian Dictionary* is found under "ITALIAN, LANGUAGE—DICTIONARIES—ENGLISH"

3. *Polyglot dictionaries* define terms in several languages and usually restrict themselves to a specific field. To locate this type of dictionary, use a subject heading such as "FORESTS AND FORESTRY—DICTIONARIES—POLYGLOT."
   Example: *Elsevier's Wood Dictionary in Seven Languages* is found under "TIMBER—DICTIONARIES—POLYGLOT"

4. *Subject dictionaries* attempt to list and define all the basic and highly specialized terms used in a particular field. Normally the definitions are more complete and up to date than those in a general dictionary. Abbreviation, jargon, slang, or terminology pertaining to a specific area are defined. To locate a subject dictionary, use the subheadings "DIC-TIONARIES," "GLOSSARY," or "TERMINOLOGY." For example: "SCI-

ENCE—DICTIONARIES"; "HORTICULTURE—DICTIONARIES"; "FORESTS AND FORESTRY—DICTIONARIES."

> Examples: *The Dictionary of the Biological Sciences* is found under "BIOLOGY—DICTIONARIES"
>
> *The Dictionary of Paper* is found under "PAPER—DICTIONARIES"

Directories

A directory is a list of people or organizations, usually including addresses and often including other information as well. Directories are primarily information-locating tools. You may use the subheading "DIRECTORIES" with your main subject when searching for most of these in the catalog. However, other subject headings should be explored. Several categories of directories are listed below, with examples.

1. *Local directories*
   Example: A city telephone directory

2. *Government directories*
   Examples: *The Congressional Directory* is found under "U.S. CONGRESS—REGISTERS"

   The U.S. Government Manual is found under "U.S. POLITICS & GOVERNMENT—HANDBOOKS AND MANUALS, ETC."

3. *Institutional directories* (usually including schools, foundations, research institutions, museums, and similar organizations)*
   Examples: *The World of Learning* is found under "LEARNED INSTITUTIONS AND SOCIETIES"

   Encyclopedia of Associations is found under "ASSOCIATIONS, INSTITUTIONS, ETC.—U.S.—DIRECTORIES"

   The Foundation Directory is found under "ENDOWMENTS—DIRECTORIES"

   Research Centers Directory is found under "RESEARCH—U.S.—DIRECTORIES"

4. *Professional directories* (primarily listing members of a profession or professional organizations such as law, medicine, forestry, or architecture)
   Examples: *The Naturalists' Directory (International)* is found under "SCIENTISTS—DIRECTORIES"

   American Architects Directory is found under "ARCHITECTS—U.S.—DIRECTORIES"

5. *Trade or business directories* (listing manufacturers' information about companies, industries, and personal services)
   Examples: *Thomas' Register* is found under "INDUSTRIES, LOCATION OF"

   Industrial Research Laboratories is found under "RESEARCH, INDUSTRIAL—U.S."

6. *Directories for particular interest or discipline*
   Example: *Conservation Directory* is found under "NATURAL RE-
   SOURCES—DIRECTORIES"

Biographical Information

Reference books compiled specifically to give biographical information are
sometimes very useful. While some biographical information is contained in
other sources (such as encyclopedias and almanacs), the coverage is usually
limited. Whether you use general or subject biographical sources, the listings
may be brief or detailed, restricted to the living or dead, or given by country.
Variation in the spelling of names is one of the problems encountered in using this
type of book. Use the subheadings "BIOGRAPHIES" or "DIRECTORIES" in the
subject catalog to locate biographical information, or use headings such as
"BIOGRAPHY—DICTIONARIES," "UNITED STATES—BIOGRAPHY—DICTIONA-
RIES."

   Examples: *American Men and Women of Science* is found under
   "SCIENTISTS, AMERICAN—DIRECTORIES"

   Dictionary of Scientific Biography is found under "SCIENTISTS—
   BIOGRAPHY—DICTIONARIES"

   Who's Who is found under "GREAT BRITAIN—BIOGRAPHY—
   DICTIONARIES"

   Who's Who in Government is found under "U.S.—BIOGRAPHY"

   Who's Who in Science in Europe is found under "SCIENTISTS—
   EUROPE—DIRECTORIES"

Atlases

An atlas is a volume of maps. Atlases and maps can be divided into two
general classes. The first is political or physical or a combination of both. The
second is thematic, which means it serves some special purpose (theme)
such as climatological, meteorological, population, and statistical. Thematic
atlases can be located using the subheading "MAPS" after a subject. For
example: "FORESTS AND FORESTRY—MAPS." General atlases can be found
under the subject heading "ATLASES."

1. *General atlases*
   Examples: *The Odyssey World Atlas* and *National Geographic Atlas of the
   World*
   Both can be found under "ATLASES"

2. *Thematic atlases*
   Examples: *A Forest Atlas of the Northeast* is found under "FORESTS AND
   FORESTRY—MAPS"

   Applachian Region of New York State is found under "NEW
   YORK (STATE)—MAPS"

Gazetteers

A gazetteer may be defined as a geographical dictionary. It is similar to the index of an atlas but is usually more comprehensive. It is a geographical dictionary of cities, mountains, rivers, and populations. Gazetteers may be located in the subject catalog, using subject headings like the following: "GEOGRAPHY—DICTIONARIES," "PHYSICAL GEOGRAPHY—DICTIONARIES."

> Examples: *The Columbia Lippincott Gazetteer of the World* is found under "GEOGRAPHY—DICTIONARIES"
>
> *A Dictionary of Geography* is found under "GEOGRAPHY—DICTIONARIES"

Handbooks and Manuals

Handbooks and manuals incorporate into one volume the most frequently needed information in a given field of knowledge. Normally they emphasize established knowledge rather than recent progress, although they are usually revised frequently.

1. *General handbooks and manuals* vary in scope and purpose but are among the few catchall sources of facts covering almost all areas of human knowledge. While the information can be found in other sources, it is likely to be buried in lengthy articles. Almanacs also fit this catchall description, although actually they are a type of reference source in their own right. Most almanacs are crammed full of every conceivable type of information. Although the information is usually sketchy, its great value is that it is up to date. Almanacs are also considered in the category of year-books. They are located in the card catalog under the two subject headings "ALMANACS, AMERICAN," and "STATISTICS—YEARBOOKS."

   > Example: *The World Almanac and Book of Facts* is found under "ALMANACS, AMERICAN"

2. *Subject handbooks and manuals* can be located under the subheadings "HANDBOOKS, MANUALS, ETC.," "STATISTICS," or "TABLES, ETC." Every field of knowledge has its own manuals and handbooks. The following are just a few examples:

   > Examples: *CRC Handbook of Chemistry and Physics* is found under "CHEMISTRY—TABLES, ETC."
   >
   > *Biology Data Book* is found under "BIOLOGY—TABLES-ETC."
   >
   > *Building Construction Handbook* is found under "BUILDING—HANDBOOKS, MANUALS, ETC."

Statistical Sources

A particular type of handbook that you will sometimes need is a compilation of statistics. These sources are usually in the reference collection. There are several compilations of statistics to begin with, which may either provide your answer or serve as a starting point in a search for statistics. They are the following:

> *Statistical Abstract of the United States* is published annually and includes statistics on the social, political, and economic functions of the United States. It can also be used as a guide to larger compilations of statistics.

> *Guide to U.S. Government Statistics* is an annual guide. A more complete guide to government-published statistics is the *American Statistics Index*, which may be found in the documents section of most libraries.

> *Statistics Sources* is another guide to compilations of statistics.

The subject card catalog serves as a guide to larger compilations of statistics. Read through the cards under your subject for titles that sound as if they contain statistical information. Then check for the subheadings "STATISTICS."

How to Locate Reference Books

The two ways of finding reference materials that have already been suggested are (1) using a literature guide and (2) using the card catalog. Headings and subheadings have been suggested in the discussion of types of materials. In addition, it is possible to find materials by *browsing* and, of course, by *asking a librarian*.

Once you are familiar with the classification system used in the library, it is possible to go directly to the shelf where you suspect reference books might be shelved and *browse*. For example, language dictionaries are shelved in the P's, pure science dictionaries in the Q's, and applied science dictionaries in the T's. Browsing in a reference collection is a good way to become aware of specific books. However, depending too much on browsing can cause you to miss several sources.

How to Use a Reference Book

There are several questions to ask about a reference book that you are using for the first time. Look it over, skim the introduction, and then ask:

1. Is my topic likely to be included in the subject covered by the book? Obviously *Agricultural Statistics* won't help you answer a question on the production of harmonicas.

2. How is it arranged? One alphabetical list by topic, or chronological?
3. Is there an index? If there is, use it. It is especially helpful when using encyclopedias to check the index, as many references can be missed if you consult only one heading.
4. Are there bibliographies or references to other sources? These may lead to information you need.
5. Is there a section which explains symbols or abbreviations? This can usually be found in the introduction or just before the text.
6. Does the date of publication indicate both currency and relevance to your topic?

Bibliography of Selected Reference Sources

This list includes reference books representative of the types described in this chapter and important to the environmental sciences. These sources may have new editions as reference books are frequently updated. Always check for the newest edition available.

Agricultural Statistics. (Annual.) U.S. Department of Agriculture, Washington, D.C.

American Architects Directory. (Annual.) R. R. Bowker, New York.

American Men and Woman of Science. (Irregular serial.) Edited by the Jaques Cattell Press. R. R. Bowker, New York.

American Statistics Index. 1973- Congressional Information Service, Washington, D.C.

Appalachian Region of New York State. 1969. New York, State Office of Planning Coordination, Albany.

Biology Data Book. 1972-74. Edited by P.L. Altman and D.S. Dittmer. FASEB, Washington, D.C.

Building Construction Handbook 3rd ed. 1975. Edited by Frank S. Merritt. McGraw-Hill, New York.

CRC Handbook of Chemistry and Physics. (Annual.) Chemical Rubber Company, Cleveland, Ohio.

CRC Handbook of Environmental Control. 1973. Chemical Rubber Company, Cleveland, Ohio. 6 vols.

The Cambridge Italian Dictionary. 1962- (in progress). Edited by Barbara Reynolds. Cambridge University Press, Cambridge, England.

Columbia Lippincott Gazetteer of the World. 1962. Columbia University Press, New York.

The Congressional Directory. (Annual.) United States Congress, Washington D.C.

Conservation Directory. (Annual.) The National Wildlife Federation, Washington, D.C.

Dictionary of Architectural Science. 1973. By Henry J. Cowan. John Wiley, New York.

Dictionary of Architecture and Construction. 1975. Edited by Cyril M. Harris. McGraw-Hill, New York.

A Dictionary of Geography. 2nd ed. 1970. Edited by F. J. Monkhouse. Aldine, Chicago.

The Dictionary of Paper. 3rd ed. 1965. American Pulp and Paper Association, New York.

Dictionary of Scientific Biography. 1970- (in progress). Editor-in-chief, Charles Coulston. Scribner, New York.

Dictionary of Scientific Directories. 2nd ed. 1972. Compiled by Anthony P.
Harvey, Francis Hodgson, Guernsey, British Isles.

The Dictionary of the Biological Sciences. 1967. By Peter Gray.Reinhold,
New York.

Dictionary of the Environmental Sciences. 1973. Compiled by Robert W.
Durrenberger. National Press Books, Palo Alto, California.

Dictionary of Water and Water Engineering. 1973. By A. Nelson and K. D.
Nelson. Chemical Rubber Company, Cleveland, Ohio.

Directory of Consumer Protection and Environmental Agencies. 1973. Academic
Media, Orange, New Jersey.

Directory of Environmental Life Scientists. 1974. Institute of Ecology for the
United States Army Corps of Engineers, Washington, D.C.

A Directory of Information Resources in the United States: Biological Sciences.
1972. Library of Congress, Washington D.C.

*A Directory of Information Resources in the United States: Physical Sciences
Engineering.* 1971. Library of Congress, Washington, D.C.

A Directory of Information Resources in the United States: Social Sciences.
1973. Library of Congress, Washington, D.C.

Elsevier's Wood Dictionary in Seven Languages. 1964. Elsevier, New York.

Encyclopaedia Britannica. 1973. Encyclopaedia Britannica, Chicago.

Encyclopedia Americana. International edition. 1977. Americana, New York.

Encyclopedia of Associations. (Irregular serial.) Gale Research, Detroit.

Encyclopedia of Chemical Technology, 2nd ed. Completely rev. 1970.
Interscience Publishers, New York.

Encyclopedia of Governmental Advisory Organizations. 1975. (Looseleaf.)
Gale Research, Detroit.

The Encyclopedia of Management, 2nd ed. 1973. Edited by Carl Heyel. Van
Nostrand Reinhold, New York.

Encyclopedia of Urban Planning. 1974. Editor-in-chief, Arnold Whittick.
McGraw-Hill, New York.

The Energy Directory. 1974. Environment Information Center, New York.

Energy Directory Update. 1975. (Looseleaf.) Special Studies Division of
Environment Information Center, New York.

Energy Management. 1973. (Looseleaf.) Commerce Clearing House, New York.

Energy Users Report. 1973-1975. Bureau of National Affairs, Washington, D.C.

Environment Regulation Handbook. 1973. (Looseleaf.) Special Studies Division
of Environment Information Center, New York.

Environment Reporter. 1970 (Looseleaf.) Bureau of National Affairs,
Washington, D.C.

Environment U.S.A. 1974. Compiled and edited by the Onyx Group.
R. R. Bowker, New York.

Environmental Biology. 1966. Compiled and edited by Philip L. Altman and
Dorothy S. Dittmer. Federation of American Societies for Experimental
Biology, Bethesda, Maryland.

Environmental Law Handbook, 3rd ed. 1975. By F. Gordon Arbuckle and
others, edited by Richard A. Young. Government Institutes, Bethesda,
Maryland.

Environmental Law Reporter. 1971. (Looseleaf.) Environmental Law Institute,
Washington, D.C.

Environmental Science Technology Information Resources. 1973. Edited by Sidney
B. Tuwiner. Noyes Data Corporation, Park Ridge, New Jersey.

Famous First Facts: A Record of First Happenings, Discoveries and Inventions in the United States. 3rd ed. 1964. By Joseph N. Kane. H. W. Wilson, New York.

A Forest Atlas of the Northeast. 1968. By Howard W. Lull. U.S. Forest Service, Northeastern Forest Experiment Station, Upper Darby, Pennsylvania.

The Foundation. Directory. (Irregular serial.) The Foundation Center, New York.

German-English Dictionary for Foresters. 1939. Compiled by Oran Raber, Southern Forest Experiment Station, New Orleans. U.S. Department of Agriculture, Forest Service, Washington, D.C.

Grzimek's Animal Life Encyclopedia. 1972. Edited by Bernard Grzimek. Van Nostrand Reinhold, New York.

Guide to Reference Books, 9th ed. 1977. By Eugene Sheehy. American Library Association, Chicago.

Guide to Reference Material, 3rd ed. 1975. Edited by A. J. Walford, Library Association, London.

Guide to the Literature of the Life Sciences. 8th ed. 1972. By Roger C. Smith and W. Malcolm Reid. Burgess Publishing Company, Minneapolis.

Guide to U.S. Government Statistics. (Irregular serial.) Prepared by J. L. Andriot. Documents Index, Arlington, Virginia.

Historical Forestry Statistics of the United States. 1958. By Dwight Hair U.S.D.A. Statistical Bulletin no. 228. U.S. Government Printing Office, Washington, D.C.

Industrial Research Laboratories of the United States. (Irregular serial.) Jaques Cattell Press, New York.

Information Resources in the Environmental Sciences. 1973. Edited by George S. Bonn. University of Illinois, Champaign-Urbana, Illinois.

International Encyclopedia of the Social Sciences. 1968. Edited by David L. Sills. Macmillan, New York.

International Environmental Guide. 1977. (Looseleaf.) Bureau of National Affairs, Washington, D.C.

International Protection of the Environment 1977. Edited by Bernd Ruster and Bruno Simma. Oceana Publications, Dobbs Ferry, New York.

The Language of Cities; a Glossary of Terms. 1974. By Charles Abrams. King Press, New York.

Literature and Bibliography of the Social Sciences. 1973. By Thelma Freides. Melville Publishing, Los Angeles.

McGraw-Hill Dictionary of Scientific and Technical Terms. 1976. Editor-in-chief, Daniel N. Lapedes. Mc Graw-Hill, New York.

McGraw-Hill Encyclopedia of Science and Technology. 4th ed. 1977. McGraw-Hill, New York.

NFEC Directory of Environmental Information Sources. 2nd ed. 1972. National Foundation for Environmental Control, Boston.

National Directory: Environmental Impact Experts, Consultants, Regulatory Agencies. 1974. By Frank L. Cross, Jr., and Susan M. Hennigan. Technomic Publishing, Westport, Connecticut.

National Geographic Atlas of the World. 4th ed. 1975. Edited by Melville Bell Grosvenor. National Geographic Society, Washington, D.C.

The Naturalists' Directory (International). (Irregular serial.) PCL Publications, South Orange, New Jersey.

New York State Industrial Directory. (Annual.) State Industrial Directories
   Corporation, New York.
New York State Statistical Yearbook. (Annual.) New York State Division of the
   Budget, Office of Statistical Coordination, Albany.
The New York Times Encyclopedic Dictionary of the Environment. 1971. By
   Paul Sarnoff. Quadrangle Books, New York.
The New York Times Guide to Federal Aid for Cities and Towns. 1971.
   By Howard S. Rowland. Quadrangle Books, New York.
The Odyssey World Atlas. 1966. Odyssey, New York.
Recreation and Park Yearbook. (Annual.) Edited by Donald E. Hawkins.
   National Recreation and Park Association, Washington, D.C.
Reference Sources in Science and Technology. 1972. By E. J. Lasworth.
   Scarecrow Press, Metuchen, New Jersey.
Research Centers Directory. (Irregular serial.) Gale Research, Detroit.
Science and Engineering Literature: A Guide to Current Reference Sources.
   2nd ed. 1976. By Harold Robert Malinoswky. Libraries Unlimited,
   Rochester, new York.
Science and Technology: An Introduction to the Literature. 3rd ed.
   Rev. 1976. Linnet Books, Hamden, Connecticut.
Statistical Abstract of the United States. (Annual.) U.S. Bureau of the Census,
   Washington, D.C.
Statistical Sources. (Irregular serial.) Gale Research Detroit.
Statistical Yearbook. (Annual.) Department of Economic and Social Affairs,
   Statistical Office, United Nations, New York.
Thomas' Register of American Manufacturers. (Annual.) Thomas Publishing
   Company, New York.
Treatise on Environmental Law. 1975. By Frank P. Grad. Matthew Bender,
   New York.
U.S. Government Manual. (Annual.) U.S. Government Printing Office,
   Washington, D.C.
The Use of Biological Literature. 2nd ed. 1971. Edited by Bottle and H. V.
   Wyatt. Anchor Books, Hamden, Connecticut.
The Use of Chemical Literature. 3rd ed. 1978. Rev. ed. Edited by R. T.
   Bottle. Anchor Books, Hamden, Connecticut.
The Water Encyclopedia. 1970. Edited by David Keith Todd. Water
   Information Center, Port Washington, New York.
Water Resources of the World; Selected Statistics. 1975. Compiled and edited
   by Frits van der Leeden. Water Information Center, Port Washington,
   New York.
Webster's New International Dictionary of the English Language. 3rd ed.
   unabridged. 1971. G. & C. Merriam Company, Springfield, Massachusetts.
Webster's New World Dictionary of the American Language. College edition.
   1976. World Publishers, Cleveland, Ohio.
Who's Who. (Annual.) St. Martins Press, New York.
Who's Who in America. (Biennial) A. N. Marquis Company, Chicago.
Who's Who in Government. (Irregular serial.) Marquis Who's Who, Chicago.
Who's Who in Science in Europe. 2nd ed. 1972. Francis Hodgson, Guernsey,
   British Isles.

The World Almanac and Book of Facts. (Annual.) Newspaper Enterprise Association, The World Almanac Division, New York.

World Directory of Environmental Education Programs. 1976. Edited by Philip W. Quigg. R. R. Bowker, New York.

World Directory of Environmental Organizations. 1973. Edited by Thaddeus C. Nzyna. Sierra Club, Claremont, California.

World Directory of Environmental Research Centers. 2nd ed. 1974. Oryx Press, Scottsdale, Arizona.

The World of Learning. (Annual.) Europa Publications, London.

Yearbook of the United Nations. (Annual.) Office of Public Information, United Nations, New York.

Chapter 9
The Bibliography

This chapter will answer these key questions:

1. How should the material found in a literature search be evaluated for inclusion in a bibliography?
2. What are the components of a complete citation?
3. What is a style manual and why is it important?
4. What are some types of bibliographies?
5. What is a scope note?

When your literature search nears its end, it is time to *evaluate* the material you have retrieved. This evaluation is the final step before you prepare a bibliography. Examine the material critically and use only that which is relevant and significant to the topic.

Evaluating an Information Source

Research, by definition, means a studious inquiry or examination, and the purpose of inquiry is to seek information. The researcher has two tasks: first, to find the information, and second, to critically evaluate it. Because of this second task, it is a good idea to develop your own critical model for judging the quality and validity of what you read, since you may be faced daily with opposing views. Although it usually takes a specialist to make this evaluation with any finality, the following discussion includes criteria that you might consider when you construct your preliminary critical model. As your expertise grows, you will probably modify and personalize this model, but in the meantime you might consider it as you are writing your papers.

First, be sure you have filled your information need both appropriately and adequately. Trying to fit information into your paper when it isn't needed presents a problem, as does trying to use information that is in the wrong form, no matter how well written it may be.

Therefore, consider what sort of information you need. Is it

- a simple fact?
- a definition of terms?
- statistics?
- a comprehensive explanation?
- a brief summary?

Now look closely at the information you have retrieved. Does it fill your need? For example, a definition of wood products will not supply wood-products statistics or vice versa. Also, when you are reading an article critically, be on the lookout for superfluous information that was used to "fill in." Note, too, how various pieces of information are used.

To evaluate the content of the article, consider the following points.

1. *Evidence.* New facts, hypotheses, or arguments must be supported by sound evidence. If you make a statement about a new fact in your paper, you will be judged by your ability to present supporting evidence. When you evaluate someone else's writing, you should put it to the same test. The information used to substantiate a hypothesis is an indication of the quality of the article. In good scientific writing some types of evidence are more acceptable than others. Good evidence must be derived by the scientific method and, if used in a paper, it must be documented. The accompanying table shows types of evidence that might be used to document a theory or an argument.

Types of Documentary Evidence and Their Acceptability

Type of evidence	Acceptability	Documentation required
Popular opinion	Poor	None
General knowledge	Poor to satisfactory	Usually none
Survey of your own	Satisfactory to good	Methodology description
Statistical information	Good	Source citation
Expert's opinion	Good	Source citation

2. *Completeness.* Information should be complete. Is enough information included so that the research can be repeated successfully?
3. *Bias.* Any bias the author holds about the topic should be clearly stated so the reader may judge accordingly (e.g., Is the author a spokesperson for a pressure group?).
4. *Currency.* Is the source current enough to be relevant for more than historical purposes? Remember, different types of searches have different standards of currency. A taxonomic search may require an extensive retrospective search, but if the subject is relatively new or is an older topic being reexamined in new light, then the source should be current and timely.
5. *Facts or interpretations.* A fact is a known datum which can be verified. It cannot be ambiguous. An interpretation is the meaning someone gives to two or more related facts. An interpretation should not be substituted for a fact. Terms such as "suggesting" or "assumed" should not be used repeatedly.
6. *Style.* The style should be smooth and uncomplicated, without vague or flowery phrases.
7. *Illustrations.* Illustrations (graphs, charts, and pictures) should be clear, easily interpreted, and a logical amplification of the text.
8. *Conclusions.* Conclusions should be logical and explicit.

9. *References.* Works cited in footnotes or bibliography should have complete citations. Some of the references should be current.

Style Manuals

A bibliography is a list of sources, often a list of books or periodicals. There is usually some reason that these items have been placed together. They may all be on the same topic (a subject bibliography). They may all be the sources cited in one paper or thesis (literature cited). They may all be by the same author (author bibliography). Sometimes the list contains no more information than author and title, in alphabetical order, although most contain more than that. A good bibliography entry should contain all information necessary for the reader to locate the original source.

When you are writing formally (whether for school, publication, or as a practitioner) you will need to follow some style when you compile your information into a bibliography. A style manual can be your guide. It indicates exactly how to arrange the elements of the bibliography (i.e., in what order the parts go—author, date, title, etc.) and shows where to use punctuation correctly within each citation.

Before you begin to put your draft into final form, check with your instructor, editor, or immediate supervisor for the style manual you are expected to follow. Many well-conceived and well-written papers have been marked down or returned for improperly placed footnotes or a scrambled bibliography. College professors frequently have strict rules about style and format, and many journals devote a page to instructions for contributors. Pick out several of the leading journals in your field and read their instructions for contributors. This is a good method for noting the style manual used in your field. Examples may be found in *The Journal of Biological Chemistry,* volume 245 (1970), pages 1-7, "Instructions to Authors." In each issue of *The Journal of Wildlife Management* there is a page entitled "Instructions for Contributors.

After reading a few journals' instructions for contributors, ask several of your professors which style manual they prefer. *Never assume* you know the style wanted, especially for publication or your thesis.

A number of style manuals outline proper methods of preparing footnotes and bibliographies. Some examples of these are:

1. American Chemical Society. 1965. *Handbook for Authors of Papers in Research Journals of the American Chemical Society.* American Chemical Society Publications, Washington, D.C.
2. Arny, Mary T. 1972. *Ecology: A Writer's Handbook.* Random House, New York, N.Y.
3. Council of Biology Editors. 1972. *CBE Style Manual.* American Institute of Biological Sciences, Washington, D.C.
4. Mitchell, J. H. 1968. *Writing for Professional and Technical Journals.* Wiley, New York, N.Y.
5. Trelease, Sam Farrow. 1970. *How to Write Scientific and Technical Papers.* M.I.T. Press, Cambridge, MA.
6. Turabian, Kate L. 1973. *A Manual for Writers of Term Papers, Theses and Dissertations.* University of Chicago Press, Chicago, Il.

7. United States Government Printing Office. 1973. *Style Manual.* GPO, Washington, D.C.
8. University of Chicago Press. 1969. *A Manual of Style.* University of Chicago, Press, Chicago, II.
9. Woodford, F. Peter (ed.). 1968. *Scientific Writing for Graduate Students: A Manual on the Teaching of Scientific Writing.* Rockefeller University Press, New York, N.Y.

Citations

Your citations should be consistent with whatever style manual you follow. Be careful not to change your word order or punctuation within a bibliography. Regardless of which manual you follow, there are some basic things which are usually required for a proper citation. Author (or editor), title, publisher, place and date of publication, and, often, number of pages, are part of any bibliographic citation for a book. Citations to journal articles include author, name of journal, volume, issue number, pages, date, and title. Both types of citation are shown in the accompanying examples.

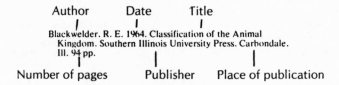

Example of a book citation

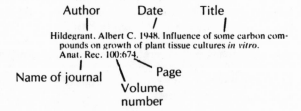

Example of a periodical citation

Compiling all your information into usable form can be a tedious task. The best method of eliminating most of the frustration is to keep careful notes of all necessary information as you go along. That way, constructing the bibliography should only require typing the information from your alphabetically arranged bibliographic cards, in whatever bibliographic style you are using. It should not require retracing your steps to locate any of the bits and pieces of information you failed to record earlier in your search.

Types of Bibliographies

If you are compiling a bibliography for a paper, you will probably include only those sources you used and actually cited in the paper. This is called a *literature cited* bibliography and it is usually arranged in alphabetical order.

A *subject bibliography* allows a little more flexibility. Think of some of the bibliographies (including indexes and abstracts) you have consulted in your search. How were some of the easy-to-use bibliographies arranged? Although the most common arrangement is alphabetical, this is not always the easiest one for a researcher to use. Think about your topic. How can you arrange it in a meaningful, logical, and useful way? Three possible ways follow.

1. Arrange the entries into subdivisions of your topic.
2. Arrange the entries in chronological order.
3. Separate entries for books and serials.

Some bibliographies contain more than a citation. They also include an *annotation* or an *abstract*. An annotation usually contains a critical comment. An abstract is a brief, unbiased summary of the original, such as those found in *Biological Abstracts*. Abstracting as a form of note-taking was discussed in an earlier chapter.

Scope Note

A well-written bibliography should contain a *scope note*. This note is a brief introductory paragraph that defines the topic, explains how the bibliography is arranged, and notes any important aspects of the bibliography.

The scope note should clearly answer any questions the reader might have about your bibliography, such as:

1. What are the writer's objectives in compiling the bibliography?
2. What does the title of the bibliography mean? For example, "The Environment," "Outdoor Education," and "Bears" are general or vague titles which should be defined more specifically.
3. For whom was the bibliography developed? College students? A citizens' environmental group? Professional chemists?
4. What time period does the bibliography cover? Is it a complete retrospective search or does it cover only the literature from 1970?
5. Does the bibliography have a particular point of view? Controversial topics—such as nuclear energy, DDT, hunting—should be clarified in terms of their particular bias or viewpoints.
6. What language(s) is (are) represented in the bibliography? Are the sources national or international?
7. What types of material does the bibliography include? Books? Serials? Government documents? Films? Other media?
8. How is the bibliography arranged? For example, why are certain subject divisions used?

These are some of the points you considered in Chapter 3 when you picked your topic and wrote a clarifying paragraph—which, it was mentioned, could be the beginning of the scope note in your final bibliography. It might be interesting to compare the two and see how much or how little you have modified your search.

Conclusion

Library Searching has presented a comprehensive search strategy and offered a number of suggestions for doing library research. This checklist offers a summary of the steps as presented in the text. Following the checklist is a brief description of four ways to conduct a short or abbreviated literature search.

Checklist for an Exhaustive Search of the Literature

I. **Learn about the library you are using.** (Chapter 2)
   A. Take a tour.
   B. How is the library organized?
   C. Ask about interlibrary loan and other special services.

II. **Select a topic.** (Chapter 3)
   A. Locate a literature summary through:
      1. An encyclopedia article.
      2. A review journal (e.g. *Advances in...*).
      3. If specific, use *Index to Scientific Reviews*.
   B. Evaluate your topic (use criteria mentioned in Chapter 3)
   C. Make a list of search terms from:
      1. Your knowledge of topic.
      2. A review article.
      3. A subject dictionary.

III. **Locate monographs on your topic.** (Chapter 4)
   A. Look up *all* search terms in *Library of Congress Subject Headings*.
   B. Follow up on relevant "sa"s.
   C. List these "accepted" terms from narrow to broad.
   D. Look up each "accepted" term in the subject catalog.
   E. Take bibliographic notes.
   F. Note new relevant terms mentioned in tracings. Add these to your list.
   G. Look up these new terms in the subject catalog and record relevant sources.
   H. Retrieve the monographs you have identified as relevant.
   I. Search the shelves (or shelf list) for sources in the area of the monographs you have retrieved.
   J. If new relevant sources are located, record the author and title.
   K. Locate these additional sources in the author/title catalog.
   L. Make bibliographic notes for new sources.
   M. Note and record the new relevant terms mentioned in the tracings.
   N. Look up these new terms in subject catalog.
   O. Repeat process until all new relevant sources are located.
   P. Check the same call numbers in additional locations. (e.g.: oversize, and reference)

Q. Search book catalogs. (e.g. NUC)

R. Reevaluate your topic.

IV. **Evaluate monographic sources** (use criteria mentioned in Chapter 4)

V. **Use indexes and abstracts.** (Chapter 5)

    A. State your search.

    B. List all search terms (descriptors) and add the following, where relevant:

        1. Subdivisions of the topic.

        2. Names of prominent researchers.

        3. Institutions.

        4. Generic names.

        5. Trade names.

    C. Determine the time period to be searched.

    D. Make a list of indexes and abstracts to be consulted.

    E. Apply the checklist discussed in Chapter 6.

    F. Search chronologically backwards through each source to be used.

    G. Keep a record of your progress.

    H. Record relevant citations on bibliographic note cards. (Noting where the citation was found.)

    I. Reevaluate your topic.

VI. **Inquire about the availability of a computer search.** (Chapter 5)

VII. **Retrieve the serials you have identified as relevant.** (Chapter 6)

    A. Decipher any abbreviations.

    B. Look up titles in author/title catalog.

    C. Locate the serials in the stacks.

VIII. **Evaluate the serial articles** (use criteria mentioned in Chapter 7)

IX. **Make use of interlibrary loan, if necessary, to retrieve sources.** (Chapter 7)

    A. Determine the ILL policies of your library.

    B. Discuss your needs with a librarian.

    C. Fill out appropriate forms for loan request.

X. **Locate and retrieve relevant government documents** (Chapter 7)

    A. Locate the government documents collection, if it is separate from the regular collection.

    B. Determine how it is organized.

    C. Use the card catalog and/or *Monthly Catalog of Government Publications* to access the collection.

XI. **Locate reference sources by using:** (Chapter 8)

    A. A guide to the Literature.

    B. The card catalog.

    C. Systematic browsing.

    D. Ask a librarian.

XII. **Evaluate all sources for inclusion in your bibliography** (use criteria mentioned in Chapter 9)

XIII. **Organize your information sources into a bibliography.** (Chapter 9)

    A. Use a style manual for correct bibliographic format.

    B. Be consistent with your entries.

    C. Write a scope note if the bibliography is to stand alone. The scope note should:

        1. Explain the writer's objectives.

        2. Amplify the title.

        3. Note audience, level, time period searched, bias, languages, types of material covered, and how it is arranged.

The Short Search

The following are examples of how you can do an abbreviated search for a limited number of sources, or how you can do a quick search when time is limited. As your expertise in searching the literature grows, so will your ability to locate information for a variety of purposes in a limited time period.

1. If you know of one or two articles on your topic, find them listed in *Science Citation Index*. This source will tell you what authors have cited your original articles. The rationale for this type of search is that articles which use your original source as a footnote are likely to be on a closely related topic. In a short amount of time, you should be able to locate several sources on your topic.
2. Locate a recent review article on your topic. To do this, use an encyclopedia article, a review journal or the *Index to Scientific Reviews*. After reading the article, locate the sources in the article's list of references. If necessary, after locating these new sources, check *their* list of references also. You should be aware that this type of search moves you chronologically back in time.
3. Locate a journal that is likely to have articles on your topic area. This can be done by consulting a source such as the subject/title index to *Ulrich's International Periodical Guide* (see Chapter 6). Locating your topic area (this particular source only indexes by very broad topics) check the list of periodicals listed. Pick one or two that your library owns. If **the** periodicals publish their own indexes (a fact that will be noted in *Ulrich's*) the search will be easier. Check the indexes of several years for each of the periodicals. If a separate index does not exist, browse through recent issues of the journal. By using this method, however, you may be limiting your references and you may also be getting a one sided viewpoint, that of one or two publications.
4. If you have a limited amount of time and want to be sure some information exists on a topic before you initiate your search, quickly scan two or three of the most relevant indexes. Determine, within a broad category, what topic has the most information. Choose that as your topic and abbreviate the rest of your search.

The four strategies mentioned above are only examples for possible abbreviated searches. The more familiar you are with the subject matter and the library tools in your field, the easier it will be to utilize the sources for your exact needs. As with any technique, the more you use it, the easier it becomes.

In any library search, whether exhaustive or abbreviated, you should keep careful notes of your steps and progress (*i.e.* a research log). When using the library, if things are not clear or problems come up, ask a librarian for assistance.

Appendix A

Selected List of Indexes and Abstracts

The following list describes indexes and abstracts that are important to the environmental sciences. For each index and abstract included, the following information is given: exact title, beginning publication date, brief description of scope and/or subject coverage; explanation of arrangement; and indication of how often the index or abstract is issued. It is important to remember that from time to time these sources make changes in their scope, arrangement, and issuing frequency. Consequently, these descriptions may become outdated.

It is helpful to examine new sources according to the checklist discussed in Chapter 6.

Abstract Bulletin of the Institute of Paper Chemistry (Vol. 1: 1931)
Abstracts of scientific and technical literature pertaining to the pulp and paper industry. Abstracts cover the theoretical principles, technologies, raw materials, products, and practices of the pulp, paper, and board-manufacturing and utilizing industries.

As of volume 37, abstracts appear in one of two sections: "Periodical Abstracts" or "Patent Abstracts." Within these sections abstracts are arranged under 40 broad subject areas as outlined in the table of contents. Cross-references are made for abstracts which pertain to more than one subject category.

Subject, author, specific name (trade names, companies, products), and patent number indexes are published monthly and annually. A keyword index is also available on a separate subscription basis.

Issued monthly.

Abstracts of Entomology (Vol. 1: 1970)
Abstracts and reference citations to insect, arachnid, and insecticide papers derived from **Biological Abstracts** and **Bioresearch Index.** The materials cover pure and applied studies of insects and arachnida including: chemical, physical, and biological controls; economic entomology; physiology; pathology; morphology; systematics; medical entomology; and ecology.

Abstracts (from **Biological Abstracts**) and reference citations (from **Bioresearch Index**) are arranged in progressive numerical order within the two major sections: "Abstracts" and "Additional Bibliographic Citations."

Each issue contains five indexes which are cumulated annually: author, biosystematic (taxonomic categories), generic, concept (formerly CROSS), and subject (permuted, keyword-supplemented titles).

Issued monthly.

Abstracts of Mycology (Vol. 1: 1967)
Compilation of abstracts and reference citations to fungi, lichen, and

fungicide papers taken from **Biological Abstracts** and **Bioresearch Index.** The material covers studies of fungi in biochemistry, cytology, genetics, microbiology (medical and industrial), pathology (plant and animal), and systematics.

Abstracts (from **Biological Abstracts**) and reference citations (from **Bioresearch Index**) are numbered progressively within their respective sections: "Abstracts" and "Additional Bibliographic Citations."

Each issue contains five indexes which are cumulated annually: author, biosystematic (taxonomic categories), generic, concept (formerly CROSS), and subject (permuted, keyword-supplemented titles).

Issued monthly.

Abstracts on Health Effects of Environmental Pollutants (Vol. 1: 1972)

Abstracts of world literature on health-related environmental pollution research. Literature is selected from **Biological Abstracts, Bioresearch Index, and Medlars.** It deals with the effects of environmental chemicals or substances on human health and analytical methods for examining biological tissues or fluids.

Entries are listed in numerical order in one of two sections: "Abstracts" or "Additional Bibliographic Citations."

Each issue contains five indexes which are cumulated annually: author, biosystematic (taxonomic categories), generic, concept (formerly CROSS), and subject (permuted, keyword-supplemented titles).

Issued monthly.

Agrindex (Vol. 1: 1975)

Bibliographic references to current literature collected from worldwide sources which are relevant to research and development in the area of food, agriculture, and allied fields.

Entries are arranged alphabetically by author within subject categories and commodity code, if the latter is given. Subject categories are as follows: agriculture; geography and history; education, extension, and advisory work; administration and legislation; economics, development, and rural sociology; plant production; protection of plants and stored products; forestry, animal production; aquatic sciences and fisheries; machinery and buildings; natural resources; food science; home economics; human nutrition; pollution; auxiliary disciplines.

Each issue contains a personal author index, corporate entry index, report and patent number index, commodities index, list of AGRIS liaison offices, and centers participating in AGRIS (International Information System for Agricultural Sciences and Technology).

Issued monthly.

Air Pollution Abstracts (Vol. 1: 1970)
Formerly **NAPCA Abstract Bulletin.**

Abstracts of selected international technical literature in the field of air pollution, accessioned by the Air Pollution Technical Information Center.

Abstracts are numbered consecutively and are arranged within the following subject categories: emission sources, control methods, measurement methods, air quality measurements, atmospheric interaction, basic science and technology, effects—human health, effects—plants and livestock, effects—

materials, economic aspects, standards and criteria, legal and administrative, social aspects, general, and miscellaneous.

Subject and author indexes are included in each issue and are cumulated semiannually.

Issued monthly.

American Statistics Index (Vol. 1: 1973)

Index to data on a specific subject plus citations for locating the original source. Indexes the full statistical output of the U.S. Government.

Sources of statistical information include: Major statistical agencies (e.g. Bureau of Census and Bureau of Labor Statistics); analytic, research, administrative, and regulatory agencies which produce statistical studies and series; and other statistical sources including congressional committees and special commissions.

ASI indexes all types of publications including: periodicals, annuals, special surveys and reports, selected journal articles, series, and statistical compilations of an encyclopedic nature.

Subject, author, categories (i.e. geographic, economic, and demographic), titles, agency, and report number indexes, are issued monthly and cumulated quarterly. **ASI Annual** cumulates the monthly supplements from the previous year.

Analytical Abstracts (Vol. 1: 1954)

Abstracts of materials dealing with all branches of analytical chemistry. Coverage includes: general analytical chemistry; inorganic chemistry; organic chemistry; biochemistry; pharmaceutical chemistry; food; agriculture; air, water, effluents; techniques; and apparatus.

Abstracts are numbered and arranged within broad subject areas as outlined in the table of contents on the back cover of each issue.

Cumulative author and subject indexes are compiled semiannually at the completion of each volume.

Issued monthly.

Applied Ecology Abstracts (Vol. 1: 1975)

Abstracts of literature in the field of applied ecology.

Abstracts are numbered consecutively and arranged under the following subject categories: methods and equipment; climate and water resources; soils; microbial, plant, and animal resources; ecosystems and their analysis; agrochemicals; pollution; and general subjects (which covers conferences to be held), research and development programs, biographies and obituaries, bibliographies, new and reprinted books, and new serials;. Abstracts are assigned to the category to which they are most relevant and cross-referenced to other sections where appropriate.

Each issue contains an author index. An annual cumulative subject index is compiled, together with a cumulative author index, at the completion of a volume.

Issued monthly.

Applied Science and Technology Index (Vol. 46: 1958)

Formerly **Industrial Arts Index** V. 1-45, 1913-1957.

A subject index to English-language periodicals in the fields of aeronautics and space science, chemistry, computer technology and applications, construction industry, energy resources and research, engineering, fire and fire prevention, food and food industry, geology, machinery, mathematics, mineralogy, metallurgy, oceanography, petroleum and gas, physics, plastics, textile industry and fabrics, transportation, other industrial and mechanical arts.

Subject entries to periodical articles are arranged alphabetically. The major section is followed by an author listing of citations to book reviews.

Issued monthly (except July). Cumulated annually.

Architectural Index (Vol. 1: 1951)

An index to approximately ten periodicals in the field of architecture.

Citations are arranged alphabetically by subject. Specific buildings are indexed under general building type and cross-filed under the heading "Architect or Designer" and location (state or foreign country).

Issued annually.

Art Index (Vol. 1: 1929)

An author and subject index to American and foreign art periodicals and museum bulletins in the fields of archeology, architecture, art history, arts and crafts, city planning, fine arts, graphic arts, industrial design, interior design, landscape design, photography and films, and related subjects.

Author and subject entries are arranged in one alphabet. Each issue also includes an author listing of citations to book reviews.

Issued quarterly. Cumulated annually.

Avery Index to Architectural Periodicals (1963 1st ed.; 1973 2nd ed.)

A subject index to the architecture periodicals of the Avery Architectural Library of Columbia University. Indexes domestic and foreign periodical articles on architecture, including: archeology, decorative arts, interior design, furniture, landscape arthitecture, city planning, and housing.

Entries appear as a photographic reproduction of catalog cards which are arranged alphabetically by subject.

The second edition incorporates the first edition and its printed supplements.

Bibliographic Index (Vol. 1: 1937)

A subject list of bibliographies which appear separately or in books, pamphlets, and periodicals. Bibliographies must have fifty or more citations to be included in the index. The index includes titles primarily in Germanic and Romance languages.

Entries are arranged alphabetically by subject.

Issued in April, August, and December. The December issue is cumulative.

Bibliography and Index of Geology (Vol. 33: 1969)

Continues **Bibliography and Index of Geology Exclusive of North America** and **Bibliography and Index of North American Geology.** Continues its numbering.

A bibliography of world literature dealing with the earth sciences.

Entries are numbered and arranged under 29 subject areas. Within each category they are arranged alphabetically by author.

Author and subject indexes are included in each issue and are cumulated annually. Until 1977 all citations as well as the author and subject indexes were cumulated annually. As of 1977 monthly citations are not repeated in the yearly cumulative volumes.

Issued monthly.

Bibliography of Agriculture (Vol. 1: 1942)

A classified bibliography listing current domestic and foreign literature of agriculture and allied sciences received by the National Agricultural Library. Coverage includes areas such as: agricultural economics and rural sociology, agricultural engineering, agricultural products, animal industry, consumer protection, entomology, food and human nutrition, forestry, plant diseases and control, plant sciences, soils and fertilizers, veterinary medicine, water resources and management.

Entries are assigned to one or more of the broad subject categories outlined in the table of contents. Within each category entries are arranged alphabetically by journal title abbreviations. Each entry is assigned an identification number, assigned sequentially throughout a volume year.

Each issue includes a list of journal titles indexed in the issue as well as the following sections: USDA publications, state agricultural experiment station publications, state agricultural extension service publications, FAO publications, and translated publications.

The following indexes appear in each issue: geographic, corporate author, personal author, and subject.

Issued monthly.

Biography Index (Vol. 1: 1946)

A cumulative index to biographical material in journals, current books of individual and collective biography, and obituaries from **The New York Times.** Biographical material from otherwise nonbiographical books is also included.

Entries are arranged in two sections. In the first one, entries are arranged alphabetically by the names of the biographees. Full name, dates, nationality, profession, and index references are given. In the second section, entries are arranged by profession or occupation.

Issued quarterly with annual and three-year cumulations.

Biological Abstracts (Vol. 1: 1927)

Preceded by **Abstracts of Bacteriology** and **Botanical Abstracts.**

Abstracts of biosciences research covering selected domestic and foreign materials. Subject areas covered include: aerospace biology, agriculture, bacteriology, behavioral sciences, biochemistry, bioinstrumentation, biophysics, cell biology, environmental biology, experimental medicine, genetics, immunology, microbiology, nutrition, parasitology, pathology, pharmacology, physiology, public health, radiation biology, systematic biology, toxicology, veterinary science, and virology. Each issue also includes lists of new books and new journals received. The latter are found under "General Biology" and the former under "New Books Received."

Abstracts are numbered consecutively and are arranged under detailed subject headings as outlined in the subject guide.

Five indexes are included in each issue: author, biosystematic (taxonomic categories), generic, concept (formerly CROSS), and subject (permuted, keyword supplemented titles). The indexes are cumulated semiannually. Issued semimonthly.

Biological and Agricultural Index (Vol. 19: 1964)
Continues **Agricultural Index (Vol. 1: 1916)**

A cumulative subject index to English-language periodicals in the fields of biology, agriculture, and related sciences. Coverage includes: agricultural chemicals, agricultural economics, agricultural engineering, agriculture and agricultural research, animal husbandry, bacteriology, biochemistry, biology, botany, conservation, dairying and dairy products, ecology, entomology, food science, forestry, genetics, horticulture, marine biology, microbiology, mycology, nutrition, pesticides, physiology, poultry, soil science, veterinary medicine, virology, and zoology.

Subject entries to periodical articles are arranged alphabetically. The major section is followed by an author listing of citations to book reviews.

Issued monthly (except August). Cumulated annually.

Bioresearch Index (Vol. 1: 1965)
A listing of research literature not included in **Biological Abstracts.** Each issue contains List of Publications Indexed, Bibliography (the main body of the index), and five indexes: author, biosystematic (taxonomic categories), generic, concept (formerly CROSS), and subject (permuted, keyword-supplemented titles).

In the bibliography section the citations are numbered consecutively and are arranged by journal source. For each citation the author, title, keywords, and pagination are given.

Issued monthly. Indexes cumulated annually.

Book Review Digest (Vol. 1: 1905)
Index to reviews appearing in selected English and American journals which are of a general nature rather than specialized. Entries are arranged alphabetically by author of the book reviewed. A brief descriptive note followed by review citations and excerpts are given for each entry.

A subject and title index is included in each issue.

Issued monthly (except February and July) with annual cumulations.

Book Review Index (Vol. 1: 1965)
Indexes reviews appearing in more than 230 U.S. and British periodicals. The reviews primarily cover the following areas: general fiction and nonfiction, humanities, social sciences, librarianship and bibliography, juvenile and young adult books.

Citations are arranged by author of the book reviewed.

Issued bimonthly with annual cumulations.

British Technology Index (Vol. 1: 1962)
A current subject guide to articles in British technical journals. Subject coverage includes the following broad topics as outlined at the beginning of each issue: general technology, applied science, engineering, chemical technology, manufactures, and technical services. This covers the pure science of manmade objects and industrial processes, instruments, and the chemistry of

individual substances. It does not include information related to agriculture or medicine.

Entries are arranged alphabetically by subject, with cross references as needed.

An author index appears in each issue.

Issued monthly with an annual cumulation.

Business Periodicals Index (Vol. 1: 1958)
Formerly **Industrial Arts Index.**

A cumulative subject index to English-language periodicals in the fields of accounting, advertising and public relations, automation, banking, communications, economics, finance and investments, insurance, labor, management, marketing, taxation, and specific businesses, industries, and trades.

Subject entries to periodical articles are arranged alphabetically.

Issued monthly (except August) with annual cumulations.

Chemical Abstracts (Vol. 1: 1907)
Comprehensive international coverage of scientific and technical materials of relevance to chemistry and chemical engineering.

Abstracts are numbered continuously through a semiannual volume. They are arranged by subject according to outlined contents, falling under one of 80 sections which, in turn, are arranged within the following categories: biochemistry sections, organic chemistry sections, macromolecular chemistry sections, applied chemistry and chemical engineering sections, physical and analytical chemistry sections.

Included in each issue are the following: keyword index, author index, numerical patent index, and patent concordance. Volume indexes include: chemical substance index, general subject index, formula index, index of ring systems, author index, numerical patent index, and patent concordance. Collective indexes published.

Issued weekly.

Chemical Titles (Vol. 1: 1961)
A computer-produced index to titles of chemical research papers. The current awareness publication includes author and keyword-in-context indexes to articles in selected chemical journals of pure and applied chemistry and chemical engineering.

Each issue is arranged in three parts. The first part is the keyword-in-context index. The second part, the bibliography, is a bibliographic listing of titles in the form of tables of contents of the journals covered by the issue. The third part is the author index, an alphabetical listing of all authors of papers covered by the issue.

Issued semimonthly.

Council of Planning Librarians Exchange Bibliography (Vol. 1: 1958)
A collection of bibliographies covering a range of topics generally related to planning. Topics covered are international in scope and widely varied, including areas such as: housing, health, social change, welfare, recreation, land use, and leisure.

Each bibliography is assigned a unique number. The bibliographies are then arranged in numerical order.

Author, key word-in-title, number, and geographical indexes are compiled cumulatively.

Several bibliographies are published each month.

Directory of Published Proceedings (INTERDOK)—Series SEMT (Vol. 1: 1965)

A bibliographic directory of published proceedings and preprints of congresses, conferences, symposia, meetings, seminars, and summer schools held worldwide, from 1964 to the present. Series SEMT covers proceedings in science, engineering, medicine, and technology.

Citations are listed in chronological order by the date of the conferences, in chrononumeric sequence.

Editor, location, and subject/sponsor indexes appear in each issue and are cumulated annually.

Issued monthly from September to June. Issues are cumulated into one volume at the completion of the volume.

Dissertation Abstracts International (Vol. 1: 1938)

Compilation of abstracts of doctoral dissertations submitted to University Microfilm International by various cooperating institutions in the United States, Canada, and a number of other countries. Beginning with volume 26, a list of cooperating universities is included, giving the dates when the institutions first began to use the service.

As of volume 27, **Dissertation Abstracts International** has been divided into two sections: (A) Humanities and Social Sciences, and (B) Sciences and Engineering. Section A covers: communications and the arts; education; language, literature and linguistics; philosophy, religion and theology; and social sciences. Section B covers: biological sciences, earth sciences, health and environmental sciences, physical sciences (pure and applied), and psychology.

Abstracts are arranged alphabetically by author under broad subject categories as listed in the table of contents.

Keyword title and author indexes are included in each issue. Cumulative indexes are issued.

Issued monthly.

EIS: Key to Environmental Impact Statements (Vol. 1: 1977)

Abstracts covering environmental impact statements. Abstracts are numbered and arranged under the following subject divisions: air transportation; defense programs; energy; hazardous substances; inland and coastal zone land use; manufacturing; parks, refuges, and forests; roads and railroads; urban and social programs; wastes; and water. Each issue includes a section titled "Impact Impressions," a short review of highlights in the issue and in the area of environmental impact statements in general.

Each issue contains subject, geographical, and agency/organization indexes. A cumulative index is also issued.

Issued monthly.

EPA Reports Bibliography Quarterly (Vol. 1: 1975)

A listing of EPA (Environmental Protection Agency) reports entered in the National Technical Information Service. The quarterly series supplements the original listing and two supplements which covered EPA reports entered in the

NTIS collection for 1973 and 1974.

Entries are arranged according to an alphanumeric accession number assigned each entry.

Title, subject, corporate author, personal author, contract number, and accession/report number indexes are included in each issue.

Issued quarterly.

ERDA Energy Research Abstracts (Vol. 1: 1976)

Abstracts published by the U.S. Energy Research Development Administration covering all scientific and technical literature originated by the organization, its laboratories, energy centers, and contractors. Coverage also includes other U.S. government-sponsored energy information; international literature on reactor technology, waste processing and storage, fusion technology; and nonnuclear information obtained from foreign governments by agreement.

Abstracts are numbered consecutively and are arranged under the following subject categories: coal and coal products; petroleum; natural gas; oil shales and tar sands; fission fuels; isotope and radiation source technology; hydrogen; other synthetic and natural fuels; hydro energy; solar energy; geothermal energy; tidal power; wind energy; electric power engineering; nuclear power plants; nuclear reactor technology; energy storage; energy management and policy; energy conversion; energy conservation, consumption, and utilization; advanced automotive propulsion systems; materials; chemistry; engineering; particle accelerators; instrumentation; explosions and explosives; environmental sciences, atmospheric; environmental sciences, terrestrial; environmental sciences, aquatic; environmental-social aspects of energy technologies; biomedical sciences, basic studies; biomedical sciences, applied studies; health and safety; geosciences; physics research; nuclear physics; controlled thermonuclear research; general and miscellaneous.

Corporate, author, subject, and report number indexes are included in each issue. They are cumulated at the end of each volume.

Issued semimonthly.

ERIC — Educational Resources Information Centers (Established 1966)

ERIC is a national information system set up to provide access to literature in the field of education. Access to the literature is provided through **CIJE (Current Index to Journals in Education)** and **RIE (Resources in Education, formerly Research in Education).**

RIE (Vol. 1: 1966) provides abstracts to report literature in education which is available on microfiche. Abstracts are numbered sequentially through the document section of **RIE.** Subject, author, and institution indexes in each issue provide access to entries. **RIE** is issued monthly with semiannual cumulative indexes.

CIJE (Vol. 1: 1969) is an index to periodical and journal literature in education. Entries are arranged alphabetically and numerically by an accession number. Access is provided through subject, author, and journal contents indexes which appear in each issue. **CIJE** is published monthly with semiannual and annual cumulations.

Ecological Abstracts (Vol. 1: 1974)

Abstracts to materials in the field of ecology.

Abstracts are numbered consecutively and arranged under the following subject categories: global and general ecology; marine ecology; intertidal and estuarine ecology; freshwater ecology; terrestrial ecology; applied ecology; historical ecology; theory, methods, and techniques.

Subject, author, and regional (geographic) indexes are published annually.

Issued bimonthly.

Education Index (Vol. 1: 1929)

Cumulative author and subject index to educational material in the English language. Areas covered include: administration; preschool, elementary, secondary, higher, and adult education; teacher education; counseling and guidance; curriculum and curriculum materials. Subject fields covered include: the arts, applied science and technology, audiovisual education, business education, comparative and international education, exceptional children and special education, health and physical education, languages and linguistics, mathematics, psychology and mental health, religious education, social studies, and educational research.

Author and subject entries are arranged in one alphabet.

Issued monthly (except July and August) with annual cumulations.

Energy Abstracts for Policy Analysis (Vol. 1: 1975)
Formerly **NSF - RANN Energy Abstracts.**

Abstracts of selected nontechnical or quasi-technical articles or reports of reference value on all phases of energy analysis and development.

Abstracts are numbered and arranged under the following subject divisions: general; systems studies and total energy; economics and sociology; environment, health, and safety, energy resources; research and development; nuclear energy; transport and storage; conservation; supply, demand, and forecasting; policy, legislation, and regulation; fossil fuels; hydrogen and synthetic fuels; electric power; consumption and utilization; unconventional sources and power generation.

Included in each issue are corporate, author, subject, and report number indexes which are cumulated annually.

Issued monthly.

Energy Index (Vol. 1: 1973)

A guide in international energy information. As of 1976, this yearbook contains a section of selected abstracts from the Environment Information Center's environmental data base, and a section which serves as the cumulative index to documents covered in **Energy Information Abstracts** for the year.

The following sections are also included in the volume: energy review (a review of the year's major events related to energy), energy legislation (in the U.S.), energy conferences, energy books, energy films, energy statistics, and a periodicals list.

Subject, SIC Code (Standard Industrial Classification Code), and author indexes follow the abstract section. Separate subject, SIC Code, geography, and author indexes follow the cumulative index section.

Issued annually.

Energy Information Abstracts (Vol. 1: 1976)
Abstracts of documents relating to energy.

Abstracts are arranged numerically in the review section of each issue under one of the following subject categories: U.S. economics, U.S. policy and planning, international, research and development, general, . resources and reserves, petroleum and natural gas resources, coal resources, unconventional resources, solar energy, fuel processing, fuel transport and storage, electric power generation, electric power storage and transmission, nuclear resources and power, thermonuclear power, consumption, residential consumption, environmental impact. Other sections included in each issue are: conferences, new books in print, and a list of periodicals covered.

Subject, industry, source, and author indexes are included in each issue. **Energy Index** now serves as a cumulative index to **Energy Information Abstracts.** Issued bimonthly.

Engineering Index (Vol. 1: 1884)
Abstracting and indexing service covering the world's engineering literature of all engineering disciplines. It covers research, development and testing, design and marketing, management, consulting, and education.

Abstracts are sequentially numbered and arranged by subject under headings selected from **Subject Headings for Engineering.** Cross-references are included.

An author index is included in each issue.
Issued monthly with annual cumulations.

Entomology Abstracts (Vol. 1: 1969)
Abstracts in the field of entomology arranged within broad subject areas: general; bibliography; systematics; techniques; morphology; physiology, anatomy, and history; reproduction and development; biology and ecology; genetics and evolution; geography and present-day faunas; and fossil forms and faunas. Sections titled "Notification of Proceedings" and "Book Notices" are also included.

Abstracts are numbered consecutively and are assigned to the subject category to which they are most relevant. They are cross-referenced to other sections where appropriate.

Author and taxonomic indexes appear in each issue and are cumulated annually together with a cumulative subject index, available at the completion of a volume.
Issued monthly.

Environment Abstracts (Vol. 4: 1974)
Formerly **Environment Information Access** (Vol. 1: 1971).

An indexing and abstracting service covering environmental information, both print and nonprint from the Environment Information Center's environmental data base. Abstracts are numbered and appear in the review section of each issue, arranged under twenty-one major envoronmental subject areas: air pollution, chemical and biological contamination, energy, environmental education, environmental design and urban ecology, food and drugs, general, international, land use and misuse, noise pollution, nonrenewable resources, oceans and estuaries, population planning and control, radiological contamination, renewable resources—terrestrial, renewable resources—water, solid waste, transportation, water pollution, weather modification and geophysical change, wildlife.

The following sections are also included in each issue: "Issue Alert," "Federal Register" (significant environmental entries contained in the source), conferences, and new books in print. Information regarding retrieval of original documents is provided. Much of the material cited is available in a microfiche collection entitled **Envirofiche.**

Each issue contains subject, industry, and author indexes. **Environment Abstracts** is cumulatively indexed annually by **Environment Index** which contains more than twice as many citations as are found in the year's issues

Issued monthly (bimonthly July-August). Issued bimonthly before 1974.

Environment Periodicals Bibliography (Vol. 1: 1972)

A guide to U.S. and foreign periodical literature in environmental and related studies.

Following a list of periodicals (those covered by the service) and a subject directory, the tables of contents of periodicals indexed are reproduced. These are arranged with broad subject categories: general, human ecology, air, energy, land resources, water resources, nutrition and health.

Each issue contains author and subject indexes. A cumulative annual index is published with the last issue of the year.

Issued bimonthly.

Essay and General Literature Index (Vol. 1: 1900)

Author, subject, and title index to essays and articles found in collections of essays and in miscellaneous works. Author, subject, and title entries are arranged in one alphabet. A list of books indexed is also included.

Issued semiannually with annual and five-year cumulations.

FAO Documentation—Current Bibliography and Current Index (Vol. 6: 1972)

Formerly **FAO Documentation—Current Index.** (Vol. 1: 1967)

Index to technical, economic, and social information in publications of the Food and Agriculture Organization of the United Nations.

Citations are arranged by accession number.

Each issue now includes an author index, subject index, index by division (of the FAO), and index by project.

Issued monthly.

Fertilizer Abstracts (Vol. 1: 1968)

Abstracts of articles from technical journals, patents, and other scientific and technical reports which cover fertilizer technology, marketing, use, and related research.

Abstracts are numbered consecutively throughout the year and appear under three main sections: technology, marketing, and use.

Each issue contains author and subject index.

Issued monthly.

Food Science and Technology Abstracts (Vol. 1:1969)

Abstracts of world literature on research and new developments in food science and technology.

Abstracts are numbered and arranged within the following 19 subject categories: basic food science (chemistry, physics, biochemistry, biophysics); food microbiology; food hygiene and toxicology; general—food economics and statistics; food engineering (equipment and processes); food packaging (materials and methods); commodity technologies—general; alcoholic and nonalcoholic beverages; fruits, vegetables, and nuts; cocoa and chocolate products; sugars, syrups, starches and candy; cereals and bakery products; fats, oils, and margarine; milk and dairy products; eggs and egg production; fish and marine products; meat, poultry, and game; food additives, spices, and condiments; standards, laws, and regulations.

Author and subject indexes are included in each issue and are cumulated annually.

Issued monthly.

Forest Fire Control Abstracts (Vol 1: 1950)

Abstracts from published material dealing with forest fire control.

Abstracts are grouped in the following eight categories: prevention, detection, presuppression, suppression, meteorology, prescribed burning, research and miscellaneous. They are numbered consecutively under each subject heading.

A cumulative subject index is prepared every two years.

Issued quarterly.

Forestry Abstracts (Vol. 1: 1939)

Abstracts compiled from world literature covering all aspects of forestry, including forest products and utilization.

Abstracts are numbered and arranged according to the Oxford System of Decimal Classification for Forestry as outlined in each issue. Subject divisions listed are: general factors of the environment, biology, silviculture, work study, harvesting of wood: logging and transport, forest engineering, forest injuries and protection, forest mensuration, increment: development and structure of stands, surveying and mapping, forest management, business economics of forestry, administration and organization of forest enterprises, marketing of forest products, economics of forest transport and the wood industries, forest products and their utilization, forests and forestry from the national point of view, social economics of forestry.

An author index and species index are included in each issue. Annual indexes include author, species, and subject indexes.

Issued monthly (quarterly before 1973).

Genetics Abstracts (Vol. 1: 1968)

Abstracts of international literature covering all aspects of molecular, viral, bacterial, fungal, algal, plant, animal, human, and medical genetics.

Abstracts are numbered and arranged under 22 major subject categories as listed in the table of contents. Each abstract is assigned to a subject area and is cross-referenced to other headings to which it is relevant. Two sections, titled "Books Received" and "Notification of Proceedings" are included in each issue.

An author index appears each month. Cumulative author and subject indexes are compiled with the completion of a volume.

Issued monthly.

Government Reports Announcements and Index (Vol. 75: 1975)
Formerly **U.S. Government Research Development Reports** which became **Government Reports Announcements.** Incorporates the **U.S. Government Reports Index.**

Abstracts of government-sponsored research and development reports available to the public through the National Technical Information Service (NTIS).

Report entries are arranged by subject group and field. Within fields they are arranged alphanumerically by an NTIS accession number.

Subjects covered include: aeronautics; agriculture; astronomy and astrophysics; atmospheric sciences; behavioral and social sciences; biological and medical sciences; chemistry; earth sciences and oceanography; electronics and electrical engineering; energy conversion (nonpropulsive); materials; mathematical sciences; mechanical, industrial, civil, and marine engineering; methods and equipment; military sciences; missile technology; navigation, communications, detection, and countermeasures; nuclear science and technology; ordnance; physics; propulsion and fuels; and space technology.

Subject, personal author, corporate author, contract number, and accession/report number indexes are included in each issue.

Issued semimonthly.

Helminthological Abstracts (Vol. 1: 1932)
Abstracts articles on helminths (parasites) to plants, animals, and humans. Since volume 39 (1970), abstracts have been divided into Series A:—Animal and Human Helminthology, and Series B:—Plant Nematology.

Abstracts are arranged numerically under subject divisions as outlined in the table of contents.

Author and subject indexes appear in each issue and are cumulated annually.
Series A—issued monthly.
Series B—issued quarterly.

Herbage Abstracts (Vol. 1: 1931)
Abstracts of research findings reported in international scientific literature on the various aspects of grasslands (natural and sown), pasture plants, and fodder crops.

Abstracts are numbered and arranged by subject according to a contents list at the beginning of each issue.

Each issue contains author and subject indexes. The indexes are cumulated annually.

Issued monthly (quarterly before 1973).

Horticultural Abstracts (Vol. 1: 1931)
Abstracts compiled from world literature on temperate and tropical fruits, vegetables, ornamentals, and plantation crops.

Abstracts are numbered and appear under the following subject categories: general aspects of research and its application; temperate tree fruits and nuts; small fruits and vines; vegetables, temperate, tropical and greenhouse; ornamental plants; minor temperate and tropical industrial crops; subtropical fruit and plantation crops; tropical fruit and plantation crops.

Each issue contains author and subject indexes. The indexes are cumulated annually
Issued monthly (quarterly before 1973).

Housing and Planning References (Vol. 1: 1948)
An index to selected publications and articles on housing and planning received by the Library of the Department of Housing and Urban Development.
References are numbered and appear under subject headings arranged alphabetically. All subject headings used are listed in the subject guide at the beginning of each issue. Each issue also incorporates a selection of books on housing and urban affairs, a list of new periodicals, and several book reviews.
Geographic and author indexes are included in each issue as well as geographic and Keywork-In-Context (KWIC) indexes to comprehensive planning reports.
Issued bimonthly.

Humanities Index (Vol. 1: 1974)
Supersedes in part **Social Sciences and Humanities Index.**
Author and subject index to periodical articles in the humanities. Coverage includes: archaeology and classical studies, area studies, folklore, history, language and literature, literary and political criticism, performing arts, philosophy, religion and theology, and related subjects.
Author and subject entries are arranged in one alphabet.
Includes a separate author listing of citations to book reviews.
Issued quarterly with annual cumulations.

Index Medicus (Vol. 1: 1960)
A comprehensive index to world literature in the field of biomedicine, including medical and health sciences, biometry, botany, chemistry, entomology, physics, psychology, sociology, veterinary medicine, and zoology. The index is the monthly bibliography of the National Library of Medicine.
Entries are arranged alphabetically by subject, each under one or more subject headings. The subject section is followed by an author section (index). A bibliography of medical reviews with its own subject and author sections is also included.
Issued monthly with annual cumulations.

Index of Fungi (Vol. 1: 1940)
A list of names of new genera, species, and varieties of fungi and lichens, including new combinations and new names, compiled from world literature. Coverage of lichens was initiated in 1971.
Names are arranged alphabetically under genera, with fungi and lichens given separate listings.
Each issue includes a host index.
Issued semiannually. A cumulative index is issued for each volume, which covers ten years.

Index to Current Urban Documents (Vol. 1: 1972)
Index to local government documents issued annually by a number of large cities and counties in the United States and Canada. Types of publications

indexed include: annual reports, audit reports, budgets, community development programs, comprehensive plans, conference transcripts, consultants' reports, criminal justice plans, demographic profiles, directories, economic base studies, environmental impact statements, evaluations and analyses, feasibility studies, inventories, surveys, manuals, minutes of proceedings, planning reports, policy statements, questionnaires, statistics, workable programs, zoning ordinances.

The index is composed of two major sections: a geographic index and a subject Index. In the geographic index citations are arranged alphabetically, first by place name and then by issuing department or agency. The subject index is arranged alphabetically by subject, and within each category entries are listed alphabetically by place name. A separate list of subject headings used by the service is available.

Issued quarterly. The final issue of each volume is published as part of the annual cumulated volume.

Index to Graduate Work in the Field of Landscape Architecture (Vol. 1: 1969)

Index to graduate research projects in landscape architecture, including references to completed theses of graduate departments of landscape architecture. Subjects covered include areas such as: aesthetics, airports, campus design, community planning, construction, design theory, diversity, floodplain management, gaming simulation, golf courses, history, historic preservation, housing, landscape analysis, mobile homes, open space, perspective drawing, planning theory, planters, power transmission lines, recreation, regional landscape design, site planning, urban design, watershed planning, and zoning.

Entries are arranged alphabetically by university, then chronologically, and finally alphabetically by author. Each entry includes a brief abstract of the work.

Each volume includes a subject index.

Issued annually.

Index to Legal Periodicals (Vol. 1: 1908)

An author and subject index to English-language articles appearing in legal periodicals of high quality and permanent reference value.

Author and subject entries are arranged in one alphabet. A table of cases, a book review index, and a list of periodicals indexed are also included.

Cumulated volumes consist of a subject and author index; a table of cases; and, since 1940, a book review index.

Issued monthly (except September) with annual and three-year cumulations.

Index to Scientific Reviews (Vol. 1: 1974)

An international, interdisciplinary index to the review literature of science, medicine, agriculture, technology, and the behavioral sciences.

The index is composed of five parts: (1) source index (an author index to the review articles covered each year, with full bibliographic descriptions); (2) citation index (a list of cited authors); (3) patent citation index (a list of foreign and domestic patents that have been cited or referred to in any current year's review articles); (4) corporate index (a list of institutions affiliated with items found in the source index); and (5) permuterm subject index (a title-word index to the review articles). In addition, a separate guide and journal list is pubished with information on coverage and format of the index plus instruction on its use.

(1) The source index is arranged alphabetically by author. (2) The citation index is arranged alphabetically by cited author. (3) The patent citation index is arranged by patent number in ascending numerical order. (4) The corporate index is arranged alphabetically by organization. (5) The permuterm subject index is an alphabetical list of significant words taken from the titles and subtitles of the review articles.

Issued semiannually and cumulated annually.

International Abstracts of Biological Sciences (Vol. 4: 1956)

Formerly **British Abstracts of Medical Sciences** (Vol. 1: 1954).

A survey of world literature in the biological sciences.

Abstracts are numbered consecutively and cover the following subject areas: anatomy, oral biology, biochemistry, immunology and experimental pathology, microbiology, pharmacology, physiology, animal behaviour, cytology, genetics, and experimental zoology. A section titled "Review Articles" also appears in each issue.

Each issue includes an author index. Annual author and subject indexes are compiled.

Issued monthly.

Key-Word Index of Wildlife Research (Vol. 1: 1974)

An index to world literature in the field of wildlife research.

The first part contains a keyword index and an author and title index which provides full bibliographic descriptions of all entries. The second part provides a list of keywords (thesaurus); an alphabetical and systematic species list with English, German, French, and Latin names of all species included in the index; and a list of periodicals covered by the service.

Issued annually.

Land Use Planning Abstracts (Vol. 1: 1974)

A guide to print and nonprint information on land use planning. The abstracts cover primarily United States related material but also include some from international sources. Information is gathered within three sections: review, abstract, index.

The review section includes: land use planning: a review, land use laws and policy, land use legislation, land use books, land use films, and land use statistics.

In the abstract section, abstracts are arranged under one of the following twenty-one subject categories, identical to those used in **Environment Abstracts,** issued by the same publisher: air pollution, chemical and biological contamination, energy, environmental education, environmental design and urban ecology, food and drugs, general, internation, land use and misuse, noise pollution, nonrenewable resources, oceans and estuaries, population planning and control, radiological contamination, renewable resources—terrestrial renewable resources—water, solid waste, transportation, water pollution, weather modification and geophysical change, wildlife.

The index section contains subject, SIC Code (Standard Industrial

Classification Code), and author indexes.
Issued annually.

Masters Abstracts (Vol. 1: 1962)
Abstracts of selected masters theses from various universities which are available on microfilm from University Microfilms.

Abstracts are arranged under 79 subject areas as outlined in the table of contents. These cover the sciences, social sciences, and humanities.

Each issue includes author and subject indexes. Cumulative indexes are available annually.
Issued quarterly.

Meteorological and Geoastrophysical Abstracts (Vol. 11: 1960)
Formerly **Meteorological Abstracts and Bibliography** (Vol. 1: 1950)

Current meteorological and geoastrophysical abstracts compiled from foreign and domestic literature. Abstracts are numbered and arranged under the following subject categories: environmental sciences, meteorology, astrophysics, hydrosphere/hydrology, glaciology, and physical oceanography. Also included in each issue is an alphabetical list of bibliographies published in Part II of Meteorological and Geoastrophysical Abstracts until 1964.

Author, subject, and geographic indexes are included in each issue. Cumulative indexes are also available.
Issued monthly.

Microbiology Abstracts (Vol. 1: 1965)
Abstracts covering world literature in the field of microbiology, divided into three separate sections: Section A—industrial and applied microbiology; Section B—bacteriology; and Section C—algology, mycology, and protozoology.

In each section abstracts are numbered and arranged under subject categories as outlined on the contents pages.

Each issue of Section A includes an author index and a patentee and assignee index which are cumulated together with a subject index at the completion of a volume. Each issue of Section B includes author and species indexes. Cumulative subject and author indexes are issued at the completion of a volume. Each issue of Section C includes author and species indexes which, together with a subject index, are cumulated at the completion of a volume.

All sections issued monthly.

Monthly Catalog of U.S. Government Publications (Vol. 1: 1895)
Supersedes a number of similar indexes of varying titles back to 1895.

A current bibliography of publications issued by all branches of the U.S. government. Entries are numbered and arranged alphabetically by issuing agency.

The following indexes are included in each issue: author, title, subject, and series/report number. Cumulative indexes are published semiannually and annually.
Issued monthly.

New York Times Index (vol. 1: 1851)
A subject index to news as recorded in **The New York Times** summarized and classified alphabetically by subjects, persons, and organizations.

Abstracts of news and editorial material are entered under subject headings and their subdivisions, which are arranged alphabetically. Entries under each heading are arranged chronologically, where date, page, and column of the item summarized are given. Related headings are covered by cross-references or duplicate entries.

Issued semimonthly with annual cumulations.

Nuclear Science Abstracts (Vol. 1: 1947)

Abstracts of international nuclear science literature of the U.S. Atomic Energy Commission and its contractors; other U.S. government agencies; other governments, universities, industrial, and research organizations.

Abstracts are numbered and arranged under the following subject categories: chemistry, controlled thermonuclear research, engineering, environmental and earth sciences, instrumentation, isotope and radiation source technology, life sciences, materials, nuclear materials and waste management, particle accelerators, (astrophysics and cosmology), physics (atmospheric), physics (atomic and molecular), physics (electrofluid and magnetofluid), physics (high-energy), physics (low-temperature), physics (nuclear), physics (radiation and shielding), physics (theoretical), reactor technology and regulation, general and miscellaneous.

Each issue includes corporate, personal author, subject, and report number indexes which are cumulated semiannually at the end of a volume number.

Issued semimonthly.

Nutrition Abstracts and Reviews (Vol. 1: 1931)

International abstracting service covering the field of nutrition, now issued in two parts(A) Human and Experimental, and (B) Livestock Feeds and Feeding.

Abstracts are numbered consecutively and arranged under the following subject divisions. Section A: technique, foods, physiology and biochemistry, human health and nutrition, disease and therapeutic nutrition. Section B: technique, technology, feeding stuffs and feeds, physiology and biochemistry, feeding and animal and diet in etiology of disease. Each issue also incorporates a section titled "Book Reviews and Reports."

Author and subject indexes are included in each issue and are cumulated annually.

Issued monthly (formerly quarterly).

Pollution Abstracts (Vol. 1: 1970)

International coverage of technical literature on environmental pollution.

Abstracts are numbered sequentially through the year and appear under the following subject divisions: air pollution, water pollution, solid wastes/waste management, noise, pesticides, radiation, general environmental quality. Each issue contains a calendar of events which lists meetings, exhibits, and conferences relevant to environmental research and pollution control.

A Keytalpha index (permuted subject index) and author index are included in each issue. Annual cumulative indexes and a five-year index are published.

Issued bimonthly.

Psychological Abstracts (Vol. 1: 1927)

Abstracts of the world's literature in psychology and related disciplines.

Abstracts are numbered consecutively through a volume and are arranged in

16 major classification categories: general psychology, psychometrics, experimental psychology (human), experimental psychology (animal), physiological psychology, physiological intervention, communication systems, developmental psychology, social processes and social issues, experimental social psychology, personality, physical and psychological disorders, treatment and prevention, professional personnel and professional issues, educational psychology, and applied psychology.

Under each subject category abstracts are arranged alphabetically by first author.

An author index and subject index appear in each issue. Full author and subject indexes are compiled for each volume (covering six months). Three-year cumulative indexes are also published.

Issued monthly.

Public Affairs Information Service Bulletin (PAIS) (Vol. 1: 1915)

A subject index to current literature in English relating to economic and social conditions, public administration, and international relations.

Entries are arranged under subject headings arranged alphabetically. Cumulative volumes include a full key to periodical references, directory of publishers and organizations, and a list of publications covered.

Issued weekly except for the last two weeks of each quarter. Cumulated five times a year, the fifth and final cumulation forming the permanent annual volume.

Reader's Guide to Periodical Literature (Vol. 1: 1905)

An author and subject index to selected United States periodicals of a nontechnical, popular character. Covers a range of scientific and humanistic subject areas.

Author and subject entries are arranged in one alphabet. A list of periodicals indexed is included in each cumulative issue.

Issued twice a month September to January and March to June; monthly in February, July, and August. Cumulated annually.

Review of Applied Entomology (Vol. 1: 1913)

International coverage of literature in applied entomology. Abstracts appear in one of two sections: Series A—Agricultural and Series B—Medical and Veterinary.

Abstracts are numbered and arranged by subject as outlined in the table of contents of each issue.

Each issue now contains author and subject indexes which are cumulated annually.

Issued monthly.

Review of Plant Pathology (Vol. 49: 1970)

Formerly **Review of Applied Mycology** (Vol. 1: 1922).

Abstracts and reviews of current world literature on diseases of plants caused by fungi, bacteria, viruses, mycoplasmas, and nonpathogenic factors.

Abstracts are numbered and arranged under subject categories as outlined at the beginning of each issue.

Author and subject indexes are included in each issue. Cumulative indexes appear annually.

Issued monthly.

Science Citation Index (Vol. 1: 1961)

An international interdisciplinary index to the literature of science, medicine, agriculture, technology, and the behavioral sciences.

This publication is arranged in five sections: (1) citation index, (2) patent citation index, (3) corporate index, (4) source index, and (5) permuterm subject index.

(1) The citation index lists all items cited in a current year. It is arranged alphabetically by cited author and then chronologically by cited year. (2) The patent citation index lists foreign and domestic patents that have been cited, arranged in numerical order by patent number. (3) The corporate index lists the organizations where work reported in the literature was done. (4) The source index is an author index to the current literature covered by the service. Full bibliographic descriptions of each item are given. (5) Finally, the permuterm subject index lists alphabetically all significant words taken from titles of the material covered in the source index.

A separate guide to the format and use of the index is published which also lists journals covered by the service.

Issued quarterly with annual cumulations.

Scientific and Technical Aerospace Reports (STAR) (Vol. 1: 1963)

Supersedes **NASA Technical Publication Announcements.**

A comprehensive abstracting and indexing journal covering current international literature on the science and technology of space, aeronautics, and supporting disciplines. Coverage includes aerospace aspects of earth resources, energy development, conservation, oceanography, environmental protection, urban transportation, and other topics of national priority.

Abstracts are arranged by accession number within the following subject categories: aeronautics, astronautics, chemistry and materials, engineering, geosciences, life sciences, mathematical and computer sciences, physics, social sciences, space sciences, and general.

Each issue contains subject, personal author, corporate source, contract number, and report/accession number indexes which cumulate semiannually and annually.

Issued semimonthly by NASA.

Selected Water Resources Abstracts (Vol. 1: 1968)

Abstracts of literature covering water-related aspects of the life sciences, physical sciences, and social sciences as well as related engineering and legal aspects of water characteristics, conservation, control, use, and management.

Abstracts are arranged within the following subject categories: nature of water; water cycle; water supply augmentation and conservation; water quantity management and control; water quality management and protection; water resources planning; resources data; engineering works; manpower, grants, and facilities; scientific and technical information.

Each issue includes subject, author, organizational, and accession number indexes. A cumulative index is issued annually in two parts: (1) Author,

organization, accession number index, and (2) subject index.
Issued semimonthly.

Social Sciences Citation Index (Vol. 1: 1973)
An international interdisciplinary index to the literature of the social, behavioral, and related sciences.

The index is arranged in the following sections: (1) citation index, (2) source index, (3) permuterm subject index, and (4) corporate address index.

(1) The citation index lists all items cited in a current year which are covered by the service. Entries are arranged alphabetically by cited author. (2) The source index is an author index to journal articles covered by the service. Each entry provides a complete bibliographic description of the article covered. (3) The permuterm subject index provides subject access to journal articles through an alphabetical listing of permuted word pairs. (4) The corporate address index is an alphabetical list of organizations which associates authors with the organizations with which they are affiliated.

Issued three times a year, the first issue covering January to April, the second covering May to August, and the third being the annual cumulative issue.

Social Sciences Index (Vol. 1: 1974)
Supersedes in part **Social Sciences and Humanities Index.**

An author and subject index to periodicals covering: anthropology, area studies, economics, environmental science, geography, law and criminology, medical sciences, political science, psychology, public administration, sociology, and related subjects.

Author and subject entries are arranged in one alphabet.

A separate author listing of citations to book reviews is included in each issue.

Issued quarterly with annual cumulations.

Sociological Abstracts (Vol. 1: 1952)
Abstracts of international literature in sociology.

Abstracts are numbered and arranged by subject under the following categories: methodology and research technology; sociology; history and theory; social psychology; group interactions; culture and social structure; complex organizations (management); social change and economic development; mass phenomena; political interactions; social differentiation; rural sociology and agricultural economics; urban structures and ecology; sociology of the arts; sociology of education; sociology of religion; social control, sociology of science; demography and human biology; the family and socialization; sociology of health and medicine; social problems and social welfare; sociology of knowledge; community development; policy, planning, forecasting and speculation; radical sociology; environmental interactions; studies in poverty, studies in violence; feminist studies.

Some volumes include supplements with abstracts of papers presented at meetings of sociological societies.

Author, subject, and periodical indexes are included in each issue.

Issued five times a year and cumulated annually.

Soils and Fertilizers (Vol. 1: 1938)

International coverage of literature in the areas of soils and fertilizers.

Abstracts are arranged according to a decimal classification outlined on the contents page, falling under the following broad subject divisions: documentation; soil science; fertilizers, soil and crop management; agricultural crops; fruit; forestry; horticultural crops; other agricultural topics; earth sciences; botany, ecology, other topics.

Author and subject indexes are included in each issue. Indexes cumulate annually.

Issued monthly.

Sport Fishery Abstracts (Vol. 1: 1955)

Abstracts of current literature in sport fishery research and management.

Abstracts are numbered and arranged under the following subject categories: aquatic plants and their control; culture and propagation; limnology and oceanography; morphology, physiology, genetics, and behavior; natural history; parasites and diseases; pollution and toxicology; research and management; reviews, bibliographies.

Each issue contains author, geographic, and species indexes. Cumulative author, geographic, species, and subject indexes are published annually.

Issued quarterly.

Translations Register - Index (TRI) (Vol. 1: 1967)

This index brings together information on the availability of English translations of serially published originals such as journals, patents, standards, etc.

The index is divided into two parts: *Serial Citation Index* and *Patent Citation Index*. The *Serial Citation Index* is arranged alphabetically by serial title with the translations arranged chronologically under each title. The *Patent Citation Index* arranges the patents alphabetically by the issuing country.

TRI is a supplement to *Consolidated Index of Translations into English* and list by subject new translations deposited at the National Translation Center, at The John Crerar Library in Chicago.

Issued monthly.

Water Resources Abstracts (Vol. 1: 1968)

Abstracts in the field of water resources for titles listed in **Hydata** (a current-awareness periodical) which are available in English in the form of abstracts.

Abstracts are numbered and arranged under 46 subject categories listed in the beginning of each issue.

No indexes.

Issued monthly.

Weed Abstracts (Vol. 1: 1953)

Abstracts compiled from world scientific and technical literature on weeds, weed control, and allied subjects.

Abstracts are numbered and arranged under the following broad subject divisions: generalia, annual field crops, grassland and herbage crops, vegetable crops, ornamentals, fruit crops, plantation crops, forests, woody weeds, aquatic weeds, other weeds, weed biology, physiology, herbicides, application, and other aspects.

Author, subject, and species indexes are included in each issue.

Indexes cumulate annually.

Issued monthly.

Wildlife Review (vol. 1: 1935)

An abstracting service covering the field of wildlife management.

Abstracts are numbered and arranged by subject under the following categories: conservation, plants, wildlife, mammals, rodents, carnivores, big game, birds, amphibians, reptiles, and invertebrates.

Each issue includes an author and a geographic index.

Wildlife Abstracts serves as a bibliography and index to abstracts in **Wildlife Review.** It includes an author index and a subject index as well as the main section "Bibliography," which is arranged by subject as outlined in the table of contents.

Issued quarterly.

World Agricultural Economics and Rural Sociology Abstracts (Vol. 1: 1959)

Formerly **Digest of Agricultural Economics and Marketing.**

Abstracts of world literature in the areas of agricultural economics and rural sociology.

Abstracts are numbered consecutively throughout a volume and are arranged under the following subject categories: agricultural economics: agricultural policy; supply, demand and prices; marketing and distribution; international trade; finance and credit; economics and production; cooperatives and collectives; education, extension and research; and rural sociology.

Each issue contains subject and author indexes which are cumulated annually.

Issued monthly (quarterly 1959-1972).

Zoological Record (Vol. 1: 1864)

A comprehensive index to the international literature of systematic zoology. Each volume is published in 20 separate sections: comprehensive zoology, protozoa, porifera, coelenterata, echinodermata, vermes, brachiopoda, bryozoa, mollusca, crustacea, trilobita, arachnida, insecta, protochordata, pisces, amphibia, reptilia, aves, mammalia, list of new genera and subgenera.

Each section is arranged in the following five parts: author index (where full bibliographic information is given), subject index, geographical index, palaeontological index, and systematic index.

Issued annually (received from two to five years after title date).

Appendix B

Glossary of Library Terms and Abbreviations

This glossary includes a list of common terms, expressions, and abbreviations used in libraries. An attempt has been made to keep the definitions as concise and clear as possible. In the case of multiple definitions, only the most common meanings, or meanings significant to libraries, are given. The following sources were consulted to compile this glossary:

Glossary. 1974. *Information*, Vol. 3, no. 4, p. 25.

Harrod, Leonard M. 1977. *The Librarian's Glossary*. Deutsch, London.

Knight, H.M. 1976. *The 1-2-3 Guide to Libraries*. W.C. Brown Co., Dubuque, Iowa.

Landau, Thomas. 1966. *Encyclopaedia of Librarianship*. Hafner, New York.

Smith, Roger. 1972. *Guide to the Literature of the Life Sciences*. Burgess, Minneapolis.

Thompson, Elizabeth. 1965. *ALA Glossary of Library Terms*. American Library Association, Chicago.

Webster's Third New International Dictionary. 1976. G. & C. Merriam Co. Springfield, Mass.

Whittaker, Kenneth. 1972. *Using Libraries*. Deutsch, London.

A. Annual

Abridgement A shortened or reduced form of a work which retains the essential character or sense of the original.

abstr. Abstract

Abstract (1). A brief summary of an article or book; (2). A form of bibliography that summarizes periodical articles or books and has adequate bibliographical descriptions to enable the originals to be found. Types of abstracts include:

　Indicative Mainly directs to the original;

　Informative Gives much information about the original, summarizing arguments and giving principal data;

　Evaluative Comments on the worth of the article;

　General abstract Covers all essential parts in an article for readers with varied interests;

　Selective abstract Condenses only parts of an article pertinent to the needs of a specific clientele;

See also **Abstract journal.**

Abstract bulletin See **Abstract journal.**

Abstract journal Periodical which contains only abstracts (for example: **Biological Abstracts**). These compilations of abstracts are frequently arranged in classified order.

Abstracting service (1) The preparation of abstracts, usually in a limited field, by an individual, an industrial organization for restricted use, or a commercial organization; (2) The abstracts being published and supplied to subscribers; (3) The organization producing the abstracts.

Accession number An inventory number assigned to a book as it is added to the library's collection.

Acronym A word formed from the initial letter or letters of each of the successive parts of a compound term: i.e., UNESCO is the acronym for United Nations Educational Scientific and Cultural Organization.

Almanac An annual publication containing a calendar and miscellaneous facts and statistics (often including astronomical data).

an. (1). Analytic, analytical; (2). Annals

anal. Analytic; analytical

Analytical entry (note) An entry in a catalog for an individual part of a work or article contained in a collection or set. Types of analytic include:

> **Author analytic** Entry under author for part of work or article within a collection.
>
> **Subject analytic** Entry under subject for part of work or article within a collection:
>
> **Title analytic** Entry under title for part of work or article within a collection.

ann. Annals

Annals Periodical publication which records events of a year, such as transactions of progress of an organization.

Annotation A note which describes, explains, or evaluates.

Annual A publication which appears once a year.

Anon. Anonymous

Anonymous Published without the author's name.

Anthology A collection of extracts of various larger works, often limited to a particular subject.

app. Appended, appendix

Appendix Additional material included at the end of a work which is supplementary to the main body of the work.

appx. Appendix

arch. Archives

Archives Organized body of records made or received in connection with the functions of a government, institution, organization, or establishment and preserved for the record-keeping purposes of that group's successors. May be collected in a separate physical location.

arr. Arranged, arrangement

assoc. Association

Atlas Collection of maps, charts, or plates, usually bound together in one volume.

auth. Author

Author Originator or writer of a work; may be an individual, a group, or an organization.

Author abstract See **abstract.**

Author/title catalog Card catalog which has cards filed under authors' names and under titles.

b. Bulletin

bibl., biblio. Bibliography

Bibliographic control The uniform identification of items or recorded information in various media, and the mechanism for gaining subsequent access to such information.

Bibliographic form The style used for arranging information in a citation or a bibliography.

Bibliography A list of writings or other materials, usually compiled on the basis of topic, author, or some other element common to the entries, and systematically arranged.

bi-m. Bimonthly (twice a month or every other month). Used in this book to mean every other month; twice a month designated here by semimonthly.

Bindery Establishment which specializes in various kinds of bookbinding.

Binding (1). The process of producing a single volume from separate parts; (2). The covers and spine of a book.

biog. Biography

Biography (1). Written account of a person's life; (2). The branch of literature concerned with the lives of people.

bk. Book

bk. rev. Book review

bm. Bimonthly (see **bi-m.**)

bull. Bulletin

c. Circa (about)

ca. Circa (about)

Call number Combination of letters and numbers which indicate where a book is located on the shelves. Call number appears on the catalog card in the upper left hand corner.

Card catalog An index to the contents of a library's collection. Each entry is in a standardized format on cards of uniform size. These cards are filed alphabetically in drawers. See also **Dictionary catalog, Divided catalog, Author/title catalog, Subject catalog.**

cat. Catalog

Catalog A systematic list of books and/or other materials which records, describes, and indexes the resources of a collection, library, or group of libraries.

Catalog card A card filed in a catalog on which an entry is made. Each card represents one item or group of materials in a library's collection. See also **entry.**

cf. Confer (compare)

ch. Chapter

Chron. Chronological

Circulation The activity of a library in lending materials to borrowers and keeping records of loans.

Citation A note or reference to a source as in a footnote or bibliography.

Citation index A list of publications which have made reference to the previously published works. The list is usually arranged so that the original reference is followed by those articles which referred to it.

Classification A systematic scheme of arrangement of books and other material according to subject or form.

Classified order Arrangement of books and other materials, or of entries in a catalog, according to a scheme of classification, frequently by subject.

Closed stacks A storage area for library materials which is not accessible to patrons. The library staff must retrieve materials.

col. Collector, colored, column

Collation Statement on catalog card indicating length or extent of work, size, and inclusion of illustrative materials.

comp. Compiler, compiled, complete

Concordance Alphabetical index of the principal words in a book or in the works of an author, with their contexts and locations.

cont. Contents, continued

Coordinate index An index which links references in such a manner as to relate all references pertinent to a particular subject. The index allows a user to find those references which share two or more common concepts of interest for a given search. i.e., see **Biological Abstracts,** Concept Index (formerly CROSS Index).

Copyright Exlusive privilege of publishing and selling a work.

Corporate author Society, institution, government, or other group responsible for the origination or writing of a work.

Cross-reference. A direction from one entry to another.

cum. Cumulative

Cumulate To combine material in earlier issues, sometimes with the addition of new material, to form a new, unified list. See also **Cumulative index.**

Cumulative index An index that combines items in earlier issues, sometimes adding new items, to form a new, unified list.

d. Date, daily; division

Data base File of bibliographic or other information.

Descriptor A subject heading or key word.

Dictionary Book containing an alphabetical arrangement of words in a language or on a subject, together with their meanings or equivalents.

Dictionary catalog Catalog in which all entries and related references are arranged together in one general alphabet.

Directory A list of persons or organizations, systematically arranged, giving addresses, affiliations, and similar data.

Dissertation A substantial paper (usually based on original research) presented by a candidate in partial fulfillment of the requirements for an academic degree or diploma.

div. Division

Divided catalog Card catalog split for convenience of user into separate sections (usually by author/title and subject). See also **Card catalog, Subject card catalog, Author/title catalog.**

do. Ditto

doc. Document

Document See government publication.

Documentation (1). Act of collecting, classifying, and making information accessible; (2). Providing bibliographic citations for documents to substantiate information.

dup. Duplicate

e.g. Exempli gratia (for example)

ed. Edited, edition, editor

Edition All copies of a book, magazine, or newspaper produced from one setting of the type.

Editor One who prepares for publication a work or collection of works not his own.

Encyclopedia A comprehensive work presenting basic information about an entire field of knowledge, usually arranged alphabetically by subject.

Entry A single record of a book in a catalog or bibliography. It consists of a heading (such as subject of author) and a description (such as the title, author, pages, publishers, etc.) of the work it is recording. See also **catalog card.**

et. al. Et alii, et alia (and others)

etc. Etcetera (and so forth)

Et seq. Et sequens, et sequentes, et sequentia (and the following)

Evaluative abstract see **Abstract**

exp. Experiment

f. Following

f.n. Footnote

fac., facsim. Facsimile

ff. Following

fig. Figure

Fortn. Fortnightly (every two weeks)

G.P.O. Government Printing Office

Gazetteer A dictionary which provides geographical information and data about places.

General abstract See **abstract**

Glossary List of terms with definitions or explanations; usually restricted to a particular subject.

Government publication (document) Any printed matter originating in, or printed with the authority (and expense) of any office of a legally organized government.

Guide to the literature Lists sources (e.g., directories and other reference works, indexes, journals) for the literature of a specific discipline or subject area. Sometimes referred to as a bibliography of bibliographies.

Handbook A one-volume compendium which treats concisely all aspects of a subject.

Heading The word, name, or phrase at the top of a catalog card to indicate some special aspect of the work (authorship, subject, content, series, title, etc.) and to bring together in the catalog related materials and materials by a single author. Entries in the card catalog are alphabetized according to their headings. See also **Subject heading.**

Holdings (1). The stock (books, pamphlets, periodicals, etc.) owned by a library; (2). The volumes, or parts of serial publications, owned by a library.

i.e. Id est (that is)

ib. Ibidem (in the same place)

ibid. Ibidem (in the same place)

id. Idem (the same)

illus., ilus., ills., il. Illustrated

Illustration Supplementary pictorial representation with a printed text (could include maps, photos, tables, diagrams, etc.)

Imprint Place and date of publication and name of publisher.

In print Available from the publisher.

ind. Index

Index A systematic list (usually alphabetical) of topics, names, etc., treated in a work, collection, or group of specified works, indicating location within the source.

Indicative abstract See **Abstract**

Indices Plural for index.

Informative abstract See **Abstract**

infra A prefix meaning below, beneath, lower, inferior.

Interlibrary loan A cooperative arrangement among libraries by which one library may borrow material from another library.

internat. International

intro. Introduction

Introduction A preliminary part of a book that states the subject and discusses the treatment of the subject in the book. See also **Preface.**

Inventory Checking the collection of a library against the shelf list to discover what material is missing from the shelves.

irr., irreg. Irregular

Issue A distinct group of copies of an edition. A single part of a volume such as issue of a journal.

Italic A variety of type with letters which slant to the right, generally used for emphasis, to indicate the title of a book or magazine, and for words in a language other than that of the surrounding text.

j. Journal

jn. Journal

Joint author Person who collaborates with one or more associates to produce a work in which the contribution of each is not separable from that of the others.

jour. Journal

jourl. Journal

Journal Newspaper or periodical, particularly a periodical issued by a society or institution and containing news, proceedings, transactions, and reports of work carried out.

jrnl. Journal

Kardex Trade name for a file where serials are recorded as they are received by a library. See also **Visible index.**

Keyword A significant word which expresses a subject, under which entries for all publications on the subject are filed in a catalog, bibliography, or index.

l. Line

L.C. Library of Congress

l.c. Loco citato (in the place cited)

Letter-by-letter filing (All through method) method of alphabetical filing where individual words are disregarded and the whole heading is considered as a sequence of letters. See also **Word-by-word alphabetizing.**

    e.g.: green acres
       green banks
       green fields
       greenford
       green howards
       greenshank

lib. Library

libn. Librarian

Librarian A specialist in the care, management, and location of recorded information and one skilled in the process of helping others locate and use information. See also **Library.**

Library An institution where diverse recorded information is stored and systematically organized and where services (such as reference assistance and circulation) are provided to facilitate its use. It may contain books, films, magazines, maps, manuscripts, microfilms, audiovisual materials, tape recordings, computer tapes, etc. It also provides information services to requesters from its own and from outside resources.

Library of Congress classification A system or classification of materials according to subjects developed by the Library of Congress for its collection. Call numbers are comprised of letters and numbers. The system allows for expansion, permitting the assignment of a unique call number for each item.

Literature Body of writings having to do with a given subject. The record of earlier work in any field is known as its **literature.** Examples would be records of observations and experiments.

Literature search Systematic and exhaustive search for published material on a specific subject together with the preparation of bibliographies and/or abstracts. See also **Reference work and research.**

Literature summary An overview or summary of the writings of a particular discipline, subject, or topic. Literature summaries are frequently issued on a regular basis such as **Annual Review or Entomology.**

ll. Lines

loc. cit., l.c. Loco citato (in the place cited)

Location symbol A letter, word, or group of letters or words used with the call-number on a catalog entry to further indicate where (in which area or collection within a library) an item is shelved.

ltd. Limited

m. Monthly

mag. Magazine

Magazine A periodical for general reading.

Main entry A full catalog entry, usually under the author, which gives all the information necessary for complete indentification of a work.

Manual See **Handbook.**

mem. Memoirs

Microcard See **Microform**

Microfiche See **Microform**

Microfilm See **Microform**

Microform General term for any of the following specific items use for storage of information:

    microcard Micro-opaque card (positive image)

    microfiche Positive or negative sheet film (usually 4 x 6 in.)

    microfilm Positive or negative roll film (usually 35mm. or 16mm.) loose or in a cartridge

Microreader A device for projecting a readable image of a microform.

misc. Miscellaneous

monogra. Monograph

Monograph Single volume dealing with single subject—a book.

Monograph series A series of monographs with a collective title, often issued by a university or society.

ms. Manuscript

n. Number

N.B. Note bene (note well)

n.d. No date

n.p. No page

n.s. New series

No. Number

Note Additional information about a book or its contents on a catalog card—for example, information indicating that a book has a bibliography.

ns. New series

Off line A term used in computerized information retrieval where computer data results are printed and retrieved after a search has been completed. (printing is usually done at a time when demand is low and computer costs are cheaper).

On line A term used in computerized information retrieval designating the direct interactive process of retrieving computer data while a search is in progress.

o.p. Out of print

o.s. Old series

op. cit. Opus citato (in the work cited); like ibid. but always preceded by appropriate author's name. Used where a citation for a different work occurs between the current citation and the previous citation for the same work.

Open entry (1). A catalog entry for a work which is not yet completed (such as a serial); (2). The portion of such an entry indicating volume or number and/or date publication began.

Open stacks Storage area for library materials. Patrons may select directly from this area.

Original source See **Primary literature.**

Out of print No longer available from publisher; stock is exhausted.

p. Page

p-slip A slip of paper 5 x 3 inches used for notes or scratch paper.

Pagination System of numbers by which pages of book are marked to indicate their order.

pam. Pamphlet

Pamphlet An independent publication consisting of only a few pages, generally less than 50.

Pamphlet file See **Vertical file.**

pap. Paper

par. Paragraph

pat. Patent

per. Periodical

period. Periodical

Periodical Publication with distinstive title issued in successive parts at regular intervals.

Permuterm index A subject index of keywords aligned alphabetically, providing multiple indexing points for significant words in the title.

pl. Plate

pm. Pamphlet

por. Portrait

pp. Pages

pref. Preface

Preface A note preceding the text of a book which states origin, purpose, and scope of the work (differs from an introduction which deals more with the subject of the book).

Primary literature Manuscripts, records, or documents of original research. Also called source material or original sources.

Printout The readable hard copy of data which has been transferred from computer tapes. It could be the result of a specific search or a list of sources stored in a data bank (i.e., a union list).

proc. Proceedings

Proceedings Published record of a meeting of a society or other organization, or a conference or symposium.

pseud. Pseudonym

Pseudonym False name used by an author.

pt. Part

Pub. Publisher, published, publication

publ. Publisher, published, publication

Publisher Person, firm, or corporate body responsible for the issuing of a book or other printed matter.

q. Quarterly

g.v. Quod vide (which see)

r. Report, reprint

Range A double-faced bookcase.

ref. Reference

Reference See **Citation.**

Reference book Book designed by its arrangement and treatment to be consulted for authoritative information rather than to be read consecutively. Also called reference work or reference source.

Reference source See **Reference book.**

Reference work (1). Branch of library's services which includes the assistance given patrons in their search for information; (2). The process of finding sources. See also **Literature search.**

rep. Report, reprint

Reprint To print again with no change in content.

rept. Report, reprint

rpt. Report, reprint

res. Research

Research An in-depth literature search which involves finding information or specific facts as well as sources.

Research log A written record of the progress and steps taken in a research project.

Research topic Subject of an in-depth literature search.

Resume A summary of the chief points of a work.

Retrospective search A search which traces literature of a subject backwards in time.

rev. (1). review) (2). revised

Revision (1). A change or correction; (2); A changed or corrected edition of a text, sometimes including supplements which update information.

s. Science

s.a. Semiannual

s.m. Semimonthly (cf. **bi. m.** Bimonthly)

sc. Science

sci. Science

Scope note Brief statement, often added to an index term or subject heading, which clarifies the range of meaning.

Search strategy The organized plan by which a person conducts a literature search.

Search term Subject heading or key word used to locate material in indexes or card catalog.

Secondary literature Sources which contain worked-over information (textbooks, encyclopedias, reviews, indexes, abstracts) and can lead to primary (original) literature.

sect. Section

See also reference A direction in a catalog or index from a heading under which entries are listed to another term or name under which additional or allied information may be found.

See reference A direction in a catalog or index from a term under which no enties are listed to the heading under which entries are listed.

Selective abstract See **Abstract**

ser. Series

Serial Publication issued in successive parts, usually at regular intervals and generally intended to be continued indefinitely (serials include magazines, periodicals, annuals, proceedings, transactions, etc.).

Series A number of separate works usually related to one another in subject, issued successively by a publisher with collective series title.

Series statement Name of a series to which a book belongs, enclosed in parentheses on the catalog card.

Shelf list A list (on cards) of the materials in a library arranged in the order of the materials on the shelves.

sic. Latin for thus, akin; used after a printed word to show that it is intended exactly as printed.

soc. Society

Source material See **Primary literature.**

Stacks (1). A series of permanent bookshelves often made of steel; (2). Room or part of a library building containing bookshelves.

stat. Statistic

Style manual A manual which ensures consistency in spelling, capitalization, punctuation, abbreviations, footnoting, and bibliographic form.

Subheading A secondary heading (or subdivision) used to divide a subject (for example, "ECOLOGY—METHODOLOGY") methodology is the subheading.

subj. Subject

Subject card Catalog card with a subject heading at the top of the card. See also **Subject catalog; Subject entry; Subject heading.**

Subject catalog Card catalog in which entries are arranged alphabetically according to assigned subject headings. See also **Subject card; Subject entry; Subject heading.**

Subject dictionary Defines terms of a particular field or of a highly specialized nature. The definitions are more complete and specific than those in a general dictionary.

Subject entry A record of an individual item in a catalog or bibliography listed under a subject heading. See also **Subject card; Subject catalog; Subject heading.**

Subject heading (1). A word or group of words on the top of a catalog card which indicates the subject matter of the entry and places similar material together. Subjects treated fully in a book are generally assigned separate subject headings. (2). A word or group of words used in an index or bibliography to locate material on a particular subject. See also **Search term.**

subscr. Subscription

Subtitle Explanatory part of the title following the main title.

Summary discussion See **Literature summary.**

supra A prefix meaning **above**

Symposium (plural: symposia) A meeting at which several researchers deliver short addresses on some phase of a topic of general interest; a collection of opinions on a subject (published).

t.c. Tome citado (volume cited)

t.p. Title page

Table of contents A list of the chapter headings and sections in a book, or articles within a periodical, usually with page numbers.

Tertiary literature Provides access to secondary and primary literature.

Text The author's work within a book as distinguished from notes, commentaries, illustrative matter, etc. (the main body or part of a book). Also a work used in classroom teaching, a textbook.

Thesaurus An authority list of words and their synonyms which accompanies a particular index to indicate the specific subject headings used in that source.

Thesis A substantial paper (usually based on original research) presented by a candidate in partial fulfillment of the requirements for an academic degree or diploma.

Title page Page at beginning of book having full title and usually the author's name and the imprint.

Tracing Record on the bottom of a catalog card of all additional headings under which the work is entered in the catalog.

trans. Translator, translation, translated, or transactions.

Transactions Published papers and abstracts of papers presented at a meeting of a learned society. Distinction between transactions and proceedings is that generally transactions are the papers of a meeting and proceedings are the records of the meeting.

Transliteration A representation of the characters of one alphabet by those of another.

Union list A record of the holdings for a given group of libraries, of material of a given type, in a certain field, or an a particular subject.

v. Verse, volume, versus

Vertical file Collection of pamphlets, clippings, and similar material arranged for ready reference, standing upright in a drawer. Often called the pamphlet file.

Visible index (1). A frame for holding cards or strips of cards on which records are entered. They are made so that all headings contained in the frame are visible at the same time; (2). A record, as of periodicals or list of subjects, contained in such a device. See also **Kardex.**

viz. Vide licet (to wit, namely)

vol. Volume

Volume All that is contained in one physical binding or designated biblio-graphic unit, such as the issues of a periodical for a given period, usually a year.

vs. Versus

vv. Verses

Weeding Practice of evaluating a collection and discarding or transferring to storage superfluous copies, rarely used books, or material no longer of use.

wk. Weekly

Word-by-word alphabetizing Arranging alphabetically with words rather than letters as units. See also **Letter-by-letter filing.**

> e.g.: green acres
> green fields
> green howards
> greenbanks
> greenford
> greenshank

y. Year, yearly

yr. Year, yearly

Yearbook Annual volume of current information in descriptive and/or statistical form, perhaps limited to a special field.

Index

References to titles of publications are not included in this index. Lists of publications appear on pages 16-18 ("Sources of Review Literature"), 76-80 ("Bibliography of Selected Reference Sources") and 91-114 ("Selected List of Indexes and Abstracts").